When Fishermen Cook Fish

When Fishermen Cook

Fish

Recipes from America's Best
and Best-Known Anglers

Rebecca Gray
and Friends

WILLOW CREEK PRESS
MINOCQUA, WISCONSIN

To my grandfather, John Glover Allbright,
who first placed a fishing rod in my hand
and patiently baited my hook.
 And to my father, Louis Lawnin Crawford,
who taught me about cooking and to never
measure too carefully . . . either in cooking
or in life.

© 1996 by Rebecca Gray

Photographs: R. Valentine Atkinson; Christine and Michael Fong.

Published in 1996 by Willow Creek Press
P.O. Box 147, Minocqua, Wisconsin 54548

For information on other Willow Creek titles,
call 1-800-850-WILD

ISBN 1-57223-067-3

Printed in the U.S.A.

Library of Congress Cataloging-in-Publication Data

Gray, Rebecca.
     When fishermen cook fish : recipes from America's best and best-
  known anglers / Rebecca Gray and friends
        p.   cm.
     ISBN 1-57223-067-3 (alk. paper)
     1. Cookery (Fish) 2. Fishers--United States. I. Title.
  TX747.G733 1996
     641.6'92--dc20
                                              96-42405
                                                CIP

CONTENTS

INTRODUCTION

I f you were about to thumb through this book looking for the 101 handy-dandy new ways to cook your man's bass, stop here — there's only a handful of bass recipes in this fish cookbook. Or, if you were looking for biographies and instructions from famous gourmet chefs, like Pierre Franey's technique for poisson meunière (sautéed fish) or Julia Childs' variation on poisson entier braisé au porto (poached fish); nope again. The famous chefs aren't here at all, and there're just a few stripped-down gourmet techniques included.

Yes, this cookbook is for cooks . . . and it's for fisherman. But it is not a listing of fish recipes. This book is designed for those who want to read good recipes authored by some very interesting, and often well-known folks who like to fish . . . or cook . . . and sometimes both.

When my husband Ed Gray and I started *Gray's Sporting Journal* in 1975 we received, as happens to newly born and formed magazines, a modest amount of "press." One of the standard questions asked of Ed during the interviews was why he'd started *Gray's*. And his stock answer was because he wanted to read it. I think if I'd been asked that same question I'd have answered, at least in retrospect, because I wanted to write for it. I've written for many other publications now about fishing, hunting, and food and always enjoyed the process. But it was the two regular features that I used to do for *Gray's* that have given me the more measurable amount of continuing satisfaction and joy. Initially I wrote biographies for *Gray's*, usually under my maiden name, on people in the hunting or fishing "business" or on people who incorporated hunting or fishing into their life in some fashion. And then for many years, I either wrote the cooking feature or worked on the food photography (or both) for *Gray's*. These experiences, these interests in the people and the food, gave direction to my inherent interests, focus to my career, and the kind of passion that assuredly will drive the rest of my life. But perhaps more directly to the point here, the blending of the two features produced the concept for this book.

This has become a really fun project, not unlike throwing a huge dinner party or organizing a church supper where the only religious talk is of trout flies and salmon runs. You scan your address book searching the names for the wittiest and most charming and talented, trying to mix and match your friends, your business associates, and some people you've heard about that have like souls. Some are painters, some photographers, editors and writers, politicians, a U.S. president, professional athlete, fishing guides, outfitters, fishing equipment manufacturers, retailers or designers — and all, all of them love to fish. You invite them to attend and bring their favorite fish dish. And what do you get? You get a great symphony of laughs, and information, envy, history, love, sadnesses, joy, satisfaction, ideas, sin and a wee bit of sexy flirtation. You get food and you get food for thought. You get this book.

And quite amazingly, in addition to their recipes the group has provided, either inadvertently or not, several running themes on food and fishing that skip helter-skelter throughout the book. These themes I, too, have written about, as have several really famous chefs: Cook fresh, cook simply, cook with flexibility; and, I would add, use wild foods — and you will cook as a gourmet. Master Chef Pierre Franey confesses that he prefers fish cookery to all others and in his book, *The New York Times 60-Minute Gourmet*, he says at the beginning of his chapter on fish "Some of the simplest dishes can be foods for the gods . . . Remember, in any of these (recipes), simply choose a fresh fish and take care not to overcook it." And later on he writes, "One of the most important things in learning to cook — and in knowing how to cook — is flexibility."

A fisherman has a tremendous advantage and is instantly on his way to gourmet chef-hood because he has the opportunity, and his very purpose is to procure a wild and fresh fish. With having a lock on wild and fresh there's then a quite natural progression to a third attribute. The invention of complex cooking techniques and involved sauces sprung from the need to cover up the taste of half-spoiled (or worse) meat and fish. So given fresh, wild fish (and the desire to get back to the fishing) the fisherman's preferred recipe mode is usually quite simple. And flexibility? Since the fisherman never knows exactly the size or maybe the species or, for that matter, even if he's going to catch a fish he must remain forever flexible. He must approximate cooking time, improvise with ingredients and the proportions, and use his imagination and senses, rather than a fixed set of rules to determine when the fish is edible.

Actually, to me, one of the truly illuminating aspects in all these different recipes is that there is a clear desire to stick to the basic simple methods: grill, poach, or fry — add some sort of fat and seasoning. But assuming the basics, then everyone improvises, however subtly. At first glance, the recipes may seem all too alike, or too vague in their instructions. I believe that slight, little nuances of change in a recipe do nothing but underscore the value of simple and basic while providing an opening to the reader's imagination, and too, provide a bit of insight into the individual's own likes and dislikes . . . as well as creates a new recipe.

My friend P.J. O'Rourke once described me as a "Martha Stewart with a gun." Well, I definitely pack a shotgun for bird hunting trips, but I hope the rest of the description is his analogical humor through the ridiculous, ha, ha. I do aspire to being M.F.K. Fisher with a fly rod. She wrote what I consider a wonderful credo, "There is a communion of more than our bodies when bread is broken and wine drunk." And I, of course, would add to bread and wine the precious taste of wild food. In the end this book is really about celebrating the natural world and about the fishermen who do that. It is stated best by the 19th century writer, Anthelme Brillat-Savarin, "Tell me what you eat, and I shall tell you what you are."

And I'd lay odds there isn't a person in these next pages who knew that's what they were doing when I asked them for a recipe.

ROBERT K. ABBETT

Bob Abbett left his successful illustration career in 1970 to paint gun dogs, fly fishing, game birds, horses and rural scenes. He is a member of the Society of Animal Artists and Who's Who in American Art and is a columnist for *Wildlife Art News Magazine*, *The Pointing Dog Journal*, and *The Retriever Journal*. In addition, his work has appear in such publications as *Sports Afield* (he was named one of the top twelve artists of America in their 100th Anniversary Issue), *Gray's Sporting Journal*, *Gun Dog*, *Southwest Art*, and *Sporting Classics*. Bob's accomplishments include the design of many popular conservation stamp/print programs including Trout Unlimited, The National Association of Bird Hunters, The Ruffed Grouse Society, The Wild Turkey Federation, and The National Quarter Horse Association, to name but a few.

Bob's interests and work have taken him to some of the world's most fabulous estates, fishing streams, kennels, and shooting preserves. He and his wife Marilyn split their time between their Connecticut farm and a studio home in Arizona where he also holds an artist's workshop annually at the Scottsdale Artists School.

Although Bob Abbett's paintings have been on the cover of several issues of *Gray's Sporting Journal*, including our Preliminary Issue, I have never actually met him. I've only spoken to him on the phone or corresponded; and so it was I talked to Bob about how he cooks and eats his fish.

"Since I was raised a Midwesterner, we were not a great fish eating family. Fishing was usually confined to family vacations 'at the lake' and the resulting pan fish, which we would then all eat with gusto, repeatedly declaring how great they were. I can remember as a kid that there were two acceptable tastes — hamburger and ice cream — everything else was iffy. But my mom was a practical cook and when she did cook fish she knew her only way of getting cooperation was by pan frying them to the consistency of a large over-cooked potato chip. Who knows what these poor fish actually tasted like. A phrase of ours which still rings in my head is 'They're not going to taste fishy are they?'

"Later in life I learned that trout, bass and catfish were marvelous if shaken in a bag with cornmeal and cooked over a campfire in the same skillet with the bacon fat. In our boating days in Connecticut, we experienced porgies, harbor blues, mackerel, and clams dug off Billy Rose's island in Long Island Sound. I think the peak though in fish eating was in Scotland: a dinner of salmon fresh from Findhorn at Altyre, the estate of our host Sir William Gordon-Cumming. I complimented his cook and told her if she came to America I'd make her a movie star."

TROUT WITH WINE SAUCE AND OLIVES

(The quantities for the ingredients were based on a 9" long fish,
     without head or tail, 1½" thick.)
1 trout, cleaned
¾ cup white wine
¾ cup chicken stock or canned chicken broth
4 tablespoons olive oil
2 tablespoons chopped green onions
1 tablespoon sliced green olives, garlic stuffed if you can find them
¼ teaspoon corn starch
Salt and pepper
Mesquite chips

Using an outside gas grill, moisten the mesquite chips and place in a pie pan under the grill and on top of the lava rocks. The fire should be started about 15 minutes prior to cooking or as long as it takes to get the mesquite smoking. (On a charcoal grill the moistened chips can be sprinkled right on the hot coals.)

Sauté the green onions in 2 tablespoons of the olive oil until they are slightly amber. Add the wine and chicken stock, salt and pepper to taste, and simmer for 10 minutes. Now add the olives and continue to simmer until the liquid is reduced by a third. Set aside and keep warm.

After removing the head and fins, wash the trout and then wipe dry. Make several vertical cuts on each side of the fish to the bone, about 1½" apart. Salt and pepper both sides of the fish and the inside cavity as well. Then paint the fish with olive oil and place on the grill. Cook for about 8 minutes per side. By not basting with the sauce as the fish cooks, the bones are more easily lifted out once the top portion of the fish has been eaten. As the fish cooks on the second side, return the wine-stock mixture to the heat and whisk in the cornstarch until the sauce thickens. Check the seasoning and adjust to taste. Serve with the trout.

BROCK APFEL

Brock Apfel succumbed to incorporating his life long love affair with fishing into his career when he joined L.L. Bean in the mid-1980s to run their fly fishing school. He writes:

"I can't remember not fishing. I grew up in Central New York, fishing as a boy near bike-accessible trout streams and bass ponds. Nobody in the family fished, nor did any of my friends — had to do it alone. I've often wondered the source of the habit. Was I born hard-wired for fishing?

"In high school I met some returning World War II veterans who introduced me to fly fishing in an organized way. From then on, through college and a stint in the Army during the Korean War, it was fish wherever and whenever I could. I knew a girl that would row the boat for me while fishing for pickerel and bass and wound up marrying her. Forty years later she doesn't row much any more.

"After graduate school it was off to the oil patch in West Texas. Long weekend drives south to the Devil's River, or northwest to the New Mexico/Arizona mountains for trout. Hard work and only fair fishing.

"After a six-year hiatus working in North Africa, we had a chance to live in commuting range of New York City. Here I was fatally smitten with the Saltwater Bug. It came in handy when we were sent for a three-year assignment in Dakar, Senegal, on the west coast of Africa. We took a boat with us and spent endless days fishing for a wide variety of pelagic species.

"Then it was back to Fun City and more Northeast saltwater fishing. There was heavy travel to the far east and Australia. I always marveled at how easy it was for a fisherman to find another fisherman in a strange land. While the language wasn't the same, there was an unmistakable bond centered on THE HABIT. A few years of that and we were off to Oklahoma for nine years. Lots of bass interspersed with trips to the coast for the salt. We bought an off-shore sportfisherman, but soon concluded that flying to the coast and driving around the ocean in a big, expensive boat with fly rods in the cockpit didn't make much sense. We sold the boat and traveled instead. Seemingly all over the U.S., to

Central America, the Pacific, and the Bahamas.

"After nine years in Oklahoma, I came to a stopping place in the oil business and we moved to Maine. In Maine we built a house on the water and had stripers and bluefish out the back door. I got involved with L.L. Bean, running a fly fishing school at first, and then developing and merchandising their fly fishing line. Numerous trips throughout the U.S. afforded a chance to be bit by the Northwestern Steelhead Bug. Many, but not enough, days on some of the compelling Oregon, Washington, and British Columbia steelhead rivers.

"After nine cold winters in Maine, we set out for Florida. And now it's tarpon, snook and redfish. Oh, my!"

B rock Apfel has been included in this book not because he worked for L.L. Bean for a few years, but because he is probably one of the very best fishermen I know. I sing his praises as a fisherman, not so much for his casting agility, although that is certainly greater than the average; or for the quantity of fish he catches, although that, too, is quite respectable. Or even for the care and skill with which he constructs his fly rods or ties his flies; I believe Brock to be a great fisherman for his soul.

Brock's passion for fishing is never compulsive, it is simply always there. This makes him not only a very good fisherman but a good fishing companion as well. I can attest to his good company from times spent with him in Alaska and Maine; but, unfortunately all a long time ago now. In recent years I have seen Brock many times over in a non-fishing context, but somehow whenever I conjure him up in my mind he is always wearing waders and holding a fly rod.

There are certain endeavors in an individual's life that are so basic, so critical to their being that there is rarely a moment when they are without it in thought, word or deed; for me this is probably cooking, for Brock it is clearly fishing. Sometimes these life forces can dominate and diminish the importance of other aspects. I admit to my fishing ability being lesser than my cooking proficiency. And Brock professes to be lacking in culinary skills. I think however, I would beg to differ somewhat with him on that count. For, not only does he understand two basic and critical elements to cooking, as he illustrates here by discussing the importance of timing and freshness; but he has discovered the ultimate in culinary alchemy. Brock has learned how to make wine from Welch's grape juice. Now that's a cook!

Brock writes, "For the expatriate oil man, life in the Kingdom of Libya in the 1960s was in many ways an idyll: Glorious climate, work hours that provided easy access to the Mediterranean, Europe just two hours away, and an American community that entertained constantly. American goods lined store shelves and the best of European and American booze and beer was stocked everywhere and sold at low prices.

"The government was run by King Idris, head of the Senusi tribe who were a strong force in the local economy. Life was pretty friendly, relaxed and good. That is, until October, 1969, when Colonel Muammar al-Qaddafi overthrew the throne and established a military dictatorship. Among the expatriates there was a general feeling of wait-and-see how life would change under the new regime.

"The wait-and-see part didn't take long at all. On about the third day of the revolution, and during an ongoing 24-hour curfew, we heard over the BBC World Service (Qaddafi used the BBC to communicate with the English-speaking expatriate community) that the good Colonel had declared the country dry in a single stroke.

"The whole country dry? No more booze? Panic! Not to worry. There are enough 'dry' oil producing countries in the world for the industry folks to have figured out how to live with it. Plans for building a home still started showing up, as did recipes for beer and wine. Sources for ingredients and flavorings were uncovered — "Kitchen Bouquet No. 23" was gin. We tried it all. Built a still, made beer, and dabbled a bit with wine. It is the wine I want to tell you about because it was where I learned how hours count when preparing something for ingestion.

"To say the least, there was not a ready supply of Gamay grapes, or any other for that matter, in Libya. So, when curfew lifted I raced to the store and bought all the Welch's Frozen Grape Concentrate I could find. On the same trip I visited a warehouse I knew to hold imported beer and found out how many cases of Amstel beer will fit in a Volkswagen beetle. A lot.

"After guessing at the strength of the grape juice and the amount of sugar and yeast, the brew was set aside to ferment. I used the fermenting time to finish building the still, and trying to figure out how to keep the dog from lifting his leg on the 50kg burlap sack of sugar we'd laid in for this work.

"We took a guess at when the wine had indeed become wine, and had a big bottling session. This was fun because, unlike distilling, where the cardinal rule is no imbibing while distilling, there is no such rule about bottling. And we got good help in the process from the folks at Amstel.

"Now this is where we learned about timing — how hours can count for a lot. We sort of understood that red wine can take 'a while' to age and become mellow. So we gave it an hour or so and cracked the first bottle. Horrible. Okay, let's wait another hour and try again; horrible (small 'h'). Now at three hours from bottling, it was not bad. At four hours it was as smooth and mellow as a merlot. We were all flabbergasted at the truly huge difference only four hours made in the enjoyability of our product.

"As a sidebar to the wine aging saga, I learned something else by doing this. In recipes, two times two does not equal four. Emboldened by my big and quick success with the red wine, I procured a 120-liter trash can and set out to make about 30 gallons of the same stuff. Multiplying the ingredients, we set the big can aside, and when done, had a big bottling ceremony. Two weeks later it had not improved beyond the capital 'H' phase.

"Years later, fishing in the Tongue of the Ocean in the Bahamas, I was again reminded how hours count. We trolled up about a 60-pound yellowfin tuna. Our guests on our boat were Jim and Barbara Richards, who together run the best home kitchen I've ever seen. Barbara suggested we stop fishing immediately and head for our villa at Chub Cay, about 30 minutes away. On the way, we cleaned the fish, cut enough steaks for the four of us, and Barbara prepared a marinade in which to drown the steaks until the charcoal was hot.

"Back at the villa the steaks got a fairly quick trip over the charcoal and onto the plate. Elapsed time, less than two hours, and it was far and away the best fish any of us have ever had. Certainly an order of magnitude better than the breakfast steaks the next morning — even though they were by any standard, excellent. They lacked the almost dreamy quality of the 120-minute versions. Here, too, hours count.

"This was reinforced a few years later when my oil career had us trapped in the mid-continent and I had to rely on largemouth bass to satisfy the cooking itch. These bass are a superb table fish; white, tasty, flaky meat. Here we had a repeat of the yellowfin experience and confirmed once again that hours count.

"My jon boat had a live-well that I could close and haul our catch home in live condition. When the grease was hot, dispatch the fish and pop it in. Another dream experience. Elapsed time maybe five minutes.

"Clearly the Chinese know what they are doing when they let you select your dinner from a tank of swimmers. That's why the best fish I've ever eaten were that yellowfin tuna, the largemouth bass and in China."

BARBARA'S YELLOWFIN TUNA

1 yellowfin tuna steak
½-¾ cup olive oil (extra virgin)
Juice of 1 lemon or the juice from 2 limes
Several dashes of Tabasco (or to taste)
2 tablespoons soy sauce
Several grinds of black pepper
1 clove of garlic, minced

Combine all ingredients and marinate the tuna steak in it for 30 minutes to 2 hours. Grill briefly.

R. VALENTINE ATKINSON

Val Atkinson is an internationally acclaimed and published photographer who specializes in angling and shooting sports worldwide. His work has appeared in *Esquire, Field & Stream, Gray's Sporting Journal, The New York Times, Newsweek , GEO*, etc. He is also a contract photographer with Frontiers International Travel and has limited edition prints that he makes available.

Val Atkinson's photography has appeared in *Gray's Sporting Journal* numerous times and, as evidenced by the use of his photos for the cover of this cookbook, I consider his work to be superb. Not only are his photographs wonderful; but he tells, in his very genuine and straight manner, an absolutely amazing — and one of my favorite — fish eating stories.

Late one night Val, his wife Susan, Ed and myself were at the Parker House Hotel bar in Boston with a group from *Fly Rod & Reel's* fishing show. The clamor from the group was to have Val tell the story about the most recent trip he'd taken on behalf of Frontiers (hunting and fishing travel agents).

Val went to Kanton Island in the South Pacific on an exploratory trip with several other professionals and a few hearty clients. Their mission was to check out the feasibility of booking the destination for bonefishing trips. Although the island was in the vicinity where the US military had done nuclear testing in the 1950s, enough time had elapsed so visiting was possible and it was thought Kanton could be the next Christmas Island. The problem was getting there; routing through the Samoan Islands or Tonga had been suspended for economic reasons so the only possible method of reaching Kanton was by infrequent boat service. Val and the group at long last got to the deserted island and quickly determined that there were indeed bonefish, but smaller-sized and further out in the ocean than expected and sort of a pain to fish for. The boat would not return for about a week (the "about" always makes importing supplies and meal planning tricky) so instead of bonefishing, the more interesting, less-troublesome, and food-wise game became trying for yellowfin tuna. On the night prior to the boat coming to fetch them, the food supply was a little past the last-meal-predictably-low level; but a 30-pound yellowfin had been caught and dinner would be festive. The fish was filleted, wrapped in cheese cloth and hung from a tree branch to keep cool in the wind à la Polynesian style. Evening faded into night, the beach fire roared and the cocktails flowed. Cooking coals had reached the perfect point and the fish was to be un-hung from the tree and brought to Val for grilling.

Val could not quite remember who exactly first saw the glowing mass of yellowfin tuna hanging, bright and illuminating from the branch. It was as if the fish had taken on the role of moon in this lunarless sky, it glowed so white and with such intense iridescence. "Boys," (long pause), "Boys!" the voice said louder now. "How long ago was it the nukes were dropped here and what exactly do we have left in the way of food?" There wasn't anything else to eat, they'd had plenty to drink, and clearly the boys were real hungry 'cause they ate the fish.

Val explained that upon returning from this ultimate eating experience he telephoned a biologist he knew at the University of California and queried the probable source of the fish's aura. The professor thought the phenomenon explainable and a natural occurrence called 'bio-illuminescense" which happens when dead flesh breaks down and creates energy. Actually, the same phenomenon has been used to explain the sighting of ghosts in graveyards. Pretty handy-dandy little explanation, I'd say.

Clearly, Val's story was not just another fisherman's tale, or an exaggeration due to the late hour or multiple after-dinner drinks — and I'm certain Val wasn't buying the professor's theory either. For when it came time to contribute to this cookbook, Val was not recommending a recipe that he used or was for a fish that could even be caught by sportfishermen. Susan buys and cooks the commercially-caught Chilean bass from the Nikko Fish Club in San Francisco, very far away from Kanton yellowfin tuna.

CHILEAN BASS

2 pounds fresh Chilean sea bass (½ pound per person)
Garlic pepper
Capers
Lemon slices (optional)

It is very important to get this fish very fresh. If you are fortunate enough to live in San Francisco, try to get Chilean sea bass from Nikko's Fish Club. It is also important to get Chilean sea bass, not Mexican or from any other place. Make certain that the piece of bass that you buy is no more than ¾" to 1" thick at the thickest part. Line the bottom of the broiler with a piece of foil. Preheat the oven on broil so it is very hot. Place the fish on the foil and sprinkle with garlic pepper, put enough so there is a light crust of pepper. Cook the fish for 8 minutes without turning. The fish should be done when the pepper is crusty and the flesh very white and slightly flaky. While the fish cooks, warm the plates and serve the bass with fresh green beans or Brussels sprouts and a nice lentil pilaff or little red potatoes.

AL BARNES

Al Barnes has been a full-time painter for the last 30 years. He has had numerous one-man shows, been the Texas State Saltwater Stamp Artist three times, the Billfish Foundation Feature Artist, I.G.F.A. Banquet Artist, National Ducks Unlimited Artist of the Year and twice the Texas Ducks Unlimited Artist of the Year. He is represented in galleries from Houston to Islamorada and Key West to Santa Fe and Honolulu.

In addition, Al is active in many conservation organizations including the Gulf Coast Conservation Association, Florida Conservation Association, Ducks Unlimited, Billfish Foundation and the Nature Conservancy. His work has appeared in many publications including *Gray's Sporting Journal* where his paintings have been the cover art more than five times..

Al spent his early career working as a commercial artist in Dallas. But he decided to return to near where he grew up on the Texas coast and has lived in Rockport for over 25 years now. He is married to a ceramic artist and they have two grown sons.

Al Barnes is a wonderful painter, primarily of saltwater wildlife, who has lived most of his life in a part of the world that was hard for this somewhat provincial New Hampshire-ite to believe could be inspirational. It's true, I envisioned the Gulf Coast of Texas as needing every few years to get purified of their oil rig platforms and trailer camps by a hardy blast of tornadoes and hurricanes.

That was until Ed returned from an assignment for *Men's Journal* on redfishing near the Matagorda and San Jose islands off Corpus Christi. Tom Montgomery had been the photographer and the pictures were stunning; beautiful long "flats" fishing shots, all sky, horizon and islands completely unmarred by civilization — lots of unique bird life and wilderness. Yes, and marshes that looked like they came straight out of a Barnes painting, because I guess they did.

And then there was the discovery of redfishing. Ed had fished places where the redfish were so plentiful that his guide, Chuck Naiser, visually likened the reddish spots flashing against the green of the underwater grasses to a "strawberry patch." Ed brought home redfish and introduced me to the Rockport, Texas, method of cooking redfish, what Chuck Naiser calls "redfish on the halfshell" and Al Barnes describes as redfish "cooked on its own platter." Whatever the title, it was superb. Previously, I'd only had redfish blackened à la Paul Prudomme style. Blackening redfish has a way of making it taste no different from any other fish, or chicken for that matter (Although Prudomme says this comes from poor blackening techniques, like cooking the fish when it's refrigerator cold or in a not-hot skillet — 600° to 700° is minimal.), but Rockport redfish leaves the fish moist and delicate with a light flavor.

With me, the popularity of a particular species of fish — whether considering its flavor or its "sportiness" — is like a large Möbius strip: It is impossible to tell at what point its popularity as food begins and the desire to catch it starts, or stops, or how the two flow together. And when you add the elements of magnificent taste and superior sportfishing qualities, you exceed mere popularity and have what is very nearly a human feeding/fishing frenzy.

Unfortunately, Ed's trip to Texas had been in absentia of Rebecca, but my redfish frenzy was soon to have some measure of assuagement. Several weeks after Ed's return we both were to travel to the east coast of Florida for an assignment I'd gotten on redfish with *Cooking Light*. Florida had just implemented its 1994 ban on commercially catching redfish and given it sportfishing status. This was long after Texas' implementation of the same laws, so there were bound to be fewer fish in Florida. Indeed, there was only one solitary fish to be caught and, of course, it was released.

Certainly more is not necessarily better. But in the case of the wonderful redfish, where the fishing is always fun and in a beautiful place, where the flavor is special and can be appreciated in a variety of ways, it would truly be nice to see those strawberry fields forever.

REDFISH (COOKED ON ITS OWN PLATTER)

1 redfish fillet, decent size and with the skin and scales left on
½ cup oyster sauce
Sprinkle of paprika
Salt and pepper
Mesquite

Paint the redfish with oyster sauce and sprinkle with salt and pepper and the paprika. Do this while the barbecue grill fueled with mesquite gets hot. Place the fish on the grill with the skin side down. Cover and cook till done (about 25 minutes) and don't turn the fish. The skin acts as a cooking tray. When the fish is done it can be easily lifted from the skin with a fork.

SAUTÉED FLOUNDER FILLETS

1-2 flounder fillets
½ cup of flour for dredging
3 tablespoons olive oil
2 tablespoons fresh chopped chives
Sprinkle of onion powder
Salt and pepper

Season the fillets with the onion powder, salt and pepper. Heat the olive oil in a skillet till hot. Cook the flounder very fast and hot in the olive oil until done, remove to plates and sprinkle on some chopped chive. Serve.

JOHN BARSNESS AND EILEEN CLARKE

> John Barsness and Eileen Clarke live on a trout stream outside of
> Townsend, Montana with a pair of Labrador retrievers. Eileen is
> the co-author of *The Art of Wild Game Cooking* (Voyager Press,
> 1996) and the author of *The Art of Venison Cooking* and *The Art
> of Game Fish Cooking*, also published by Voyager and available in
> 1997. Her articles have appeared in *Gray's Sporting Journal* as
> well as several national magazines. Her first novel, *The Queen of
> the Legal Tender Saloon*, was also published in 1996.
>
> John is a former staff writer for *Field & Stream* and presently
> the editor of *Gray's Sporting Journal*. He is also the optics colum-
> nist for *Petersen's Hunting*. He writes about hunting, fishing,
> Western history and sporting firearms for a number of magazines
> from *Big Sky Journal* to *Wyoming Wildlife*. John's most recent
> book is *The Life of the Hunt*, a collection of his outdoor adven-
> tures from the Arctic to Africa.

John Barsness and Eileen Clarke both contributed to *Gray's Sporting
Journal* while Ed and I owned it. Before our extrication in 1991,
John had some 13 articles in *Gray's*; certainly within the top five
most frequently published of the writers edited by Ed Gray. Eileen was
represented through her photography and then, after we left, she had several food features in *Gray's*. I like to believe that her post-Gray appear-
ance as a food writer in the *Journal* was unfortunate happenstance; rather
than the fact that her competition for cooking feature writer was with
someone named Gray, who had a particular *in* with Editor Gray.

Both John and Eileen are good at what they do. And there is a certain amount of satisfaction in the knowledge that a strong writer from our
time of management coupled with a talented writer-wife is now back editing *Gray's Sporting Journal*. I hope John's mouse touches the copy icon
from our era more than once while editor of *Gray's*. And for my vote, I'd
suggest if there is to be a name change it become *Clarke's Sporting*

Journal rather than *Barsness Sporting Journal.* Just for the sake of lyrical symmetry, certainly not because of the story he wrote below about his name.

"Barsness is a corruption of Bjorn's Ness, ness meaning peninsula in Norwegian. (Though some say the name comes from my great-grandfather who, upon landing in New York City, headed directly to a tavern, and after a tall ale, proclaimed, "By golly, this bar's nice!") Like any good Norski, I really like fish, especially smoked or pickled. When I was young and poor and living in the enlightened state of Wyoming, where most trout streams are legal to fish year-round, I ate a lot of Rocky Mountain whitefish, especially in winter, when they're most easily caught.

"Whitefish are traditionally smoked, but I was living in a small apartment and instead decided to pickle a few. The main ingredient of the vinegar is acetic acid, also the by-product of smoking, so I figured the whitefish would be flattered. In winter, Norwegians often make a cold pickle. Apple cider or malt vinegar works nicely, flavored with tangy root crops like red onion and garlic."

NORWEGIAN PICKLED WHITEFISH

1 average Rocky Mountain whitefish, 12" to 14" long, gutted and
    beheaded, rinsed and cut into 2 or 3 chunks
1 cup vinegar
½ medium red onion, sliced
1-2 garlic cloves, crushed
½ teaspoon salt
12 whole peppercorns
1 bay leaf

In a small pot, boil the vinegar with all the ingredients except the onion and fish. Once the vinegar mixture has been brought to a boil, remove it from the heat and let cool. Place the onions and fish in a pint-size canning jar, then pour in the cooled vinegar mixture. Marinate in the refrigerator at least 24 hours. It gets better after a week, though, and will keep for a month or two. The longer it ages the more easily the skin and bones can be pulled away from the meat; some people prefer to pickle fillets. Serve on sourdough or rye bread with a stout mustard.

I have not read any of Eileen's cookbook's but if this recipe below is any indication it is a good thing I had an in with the editor at *Gray's Sporting Journal*. It is quite good . . . and we certainly agree about butter, garlic and Madeira.

"I used to say you could eat anything if you put enough butter and garlic on it — mushrooms being a perfect example. But now I know there's one other thing that makes almost anything not only palatable but delicious: Madeira. Cooked, the complex and rich taste it imparts to the food reminds me of the resonant back beat of a bass fiddle. Hence Basso bass. And because this dish swims in Madeira, you can serve it to people — and children — who hate fish." (The alcohol in the Madeira does cook off so you need not fear inebriating your children.)

BASSO BASS

4 tablespoons butter
⅛ teaspoon curry powder
¾ cup mushrooms, sliced
2 shallots, minced
½ cup onions, finely chopped
⅓ cup Madeira wine
½ pound bass fillet, cut into 1" chunks
1 egg yolk, beaten
½ cup fish stock or bottled clam juice

Melt the butter in an 8" skillet. Add the curry powder and when you smell that, bring the temperature up to medium and sauté the mushrooms, shallots, and onions together until tender; about 5 minutes. Add the wine and diced bass and stir, coating the bass. Simmer 5 minutes. Now add the lightly beaten egg yolk and fish stock to the pan and bring back to a simmer. Cook for 2 minutes more or until the liquid has thickened. Serve immediately over rice.

STEVE BODIO AND LIBBY FRISHMAN

Steve Bodio is a full-time writer, an old-fashioned naturalist and a sportsman. Born and educated in Boston, Massachusetts, he has lived the last 16 years in Magdelena, New Mexico and considers himself "a westerner, whatever that means."

Steve has been an editor of such diverse publications as *English Literary Renaissance* and *Gray's Sporting Journal*, and he wrote a book review column for *Gray's* for 12 years. He has reviewed everything from novels to natural history in publications like *Boston's Real Paper, Albuquerque Journal, Bloomsbury Review, London's Times Literary Supplement*, and *Fly Rod & Reel*. His articles have appeared in numerous publications, including *Smithsonian, Sports Afield, Sports Illustrated, Northern Lights*, and such literary quarterlies as *CutBank*, and *Redneck Review*. He is a contributing editor to *Fly Rod & Reel, Sports Afield*, and *Shooting Sportsman* and has a column in *Big Sky Journal*.

He has been a resident faculty member at Sterling College's Wildbranch Writers Workshop in Vermont, which he founded with novelist E.A. Proulx. He currently is working on a book about the Kazakh horsemen of Mongolia and a biography of the English zoologist and artist Jonathan Kingdon.

Steve's work has appeared in seven different anthologies and he has authored eight books including: *A Rage for Falcons*, Lyons & Burford, 1984; *Good Guns*, Lyons & Burford, 1986; and *Querencia*, Clarke City Press, 1990.

Steve is a widower who, since the early 1990s, has been part-nered with Libby Frishman. Libby is currently working as the operations manger of Patagonia Mail Order. She has been an Outward Bound instructor, an archeologist, and a professional cook. Steve reports, "Libby is the only person I've ever known who was once deported from Mexico for being an illegal alien(cooking on raft trips based in Puerta Vallarta)."

S teve Bodio is the most intense person I know. This perception could be somewhat distorted because strangely enough, in the nearly 20 years since I met Steve, it has always been during the most intense times that we've been with each other — the lung cancer death of his wife, turning points at *Gray's Sporting Journal*, through love affairs (his), financial crises (his and mine) and most of the other dramas that constitute "living." Intensity can be a very difficult characteristic to deal with but, of course, it can also be very good. In Steve's case when it is good, it is very, very good because it translates to extraordinary passion. I've seen Steve feel intense passion for his falcons, for his shotguns, for the women in his life, and for books. The book passion has made him a voracious reader (and that understates it), a reader who is compelled to read everything and anything and he does just that — reads everything, yes, even cookbooks. This, combined with taste and smarts, makes him a superb literary critic.

Steve has ascribed much of his intensity to his Italian blood. One element surely carried in that Italian blood is a passion for great food and cooking. And his tastes, as exemplified in the recipes below, run to hot, of course. I guess I must conclude that Steve is intense all the time; and although I've never met Libby, it is certain that she has a good idea of how to live with such intensity — she certainly knows how to make a mean green chili . . . and more.

"This recipe originated on Outward Bound sea kayaking courses in the 1970s. We took up to twenty students island hopping and touring the coast with minimal supplies — oil, flour, chilies and tomatoes, onions and garlic, coffee, limes, spice kits and a few other basics. We taught the students to fish from their kayaks and to dive using pole spears to catch their dinner.

"The following is more of a concept than a recipe, and is definitely variable depending on what is on hand. It needed a name so we called it Baja Tacos. It is best with fresh fish, but frozen fish works also. It is also a good way to use up leftovers."

BAJA TACOS

3-4 cups cooked fish (halibut, snapper, shark, swordfish, cod, tuna,
    any dense-flesh fish will work, even shrimp or lobster)
2-3 stalks celery, chopped
3 green onions, chopped
3 Roma tomatoes, chopped
1 sweet pepper, chopped
1- 2 fresh limes
(Other suggestions to add: sliced black olives, chopped water chest-
    nuts, and/or chopped cilantro)

If you can use fish that has been cooked on the grill that is preferable as the smoky taste is delicious. Combine all ingredients and squeeze 1 or 2 limes, depending how juicy they are, over the mixture. Mix well, being careful not to mash it — you want fish pieces, not fish paste. Some people like to add mayonnaise, but I prefer it without.
Use the mixture in the following ways:
1. Tacos: Use flour or corn tortillas as you prefer. Heat the tortillas to soften them and roll the fish mixture up in them. Or quick fry the tortillas in oil, folding in half to make a crisp boat, fill with the fish mixture and top with grated cheese, salsa and fresh avocado slices.
2. Tostados: Fry either corn or flour tortillas until crispy and lightly browned. Drain and allow to cool. (The draining is important because hot oil sometimes gets trapped in the pockets of the tortillas and can really burn one's mouth — this is personal experience speaking.) When cooled, cover the tortillas with either chopped lettuce or cabbage. Put a pile of the fish mixture on the lettuce and top with salsa. You can also use home-made thousand island dressing.
3. Enchiladas: If you want to serve a hot meal; soften tortillas by heating them until pliable but not crisp, no more than 2 to 3 seconds per side. Place 2 to 3 tablespoons of the fish mixture in the center of each tortilla, add a bit of shredded cheese and sliced olives if you have them, and roll up. Grease a baking dish and arrange the enchiladas in it, side by side. Cover with green chile (Ortega or Old Paso brands are fine to use but of course, fresh roasted ones are best.), top with grated cheese and bake at 350° for 30 to 40 minutes until bubbling around the edges and warm throughout.

To make your own green chili:

If using fresh chilies: Over a direct heat blacken the skins of 12 to 15 chilies (The smoother, non-ridged ones peel more easily than the ones with irregular surfaces.). Put in a plastic bag to sweat for 15 minutes. Scrape off the blackened skins; running water can make this easier. Remove the stems and seeds. Chop. (If you don't use the fresh chilies, you'll need 2 to 3 cans.). Now chop 2 medium or 1 large onion and soften in oil over medium heat in a sauce pan. When soft add the chopped chilies, 4 to 6 cloves of chopped garlic, and cook for a few minutes. Sprinkle 2 to 3 tablespoons over the chile/onion mixture and cook 5 minutes more, making sure it doesn't stick. Add 2 to 3 cups chicken broth and stir until smooth. Season with 2 to 3 teaspoons of cumin and 1 teaspoon oregano. Adjust the seasoning with salt and pepper and more cumin if desired. You can also add 2 to 3 chopped Roma tomatoes at this point. Simmer for 15 to 20 minutes to blend flavors, cover enchiladas and bake.

SKIP BRITTENHAM AND HEATHER THOMAS

Skip Brittenham and Heather Thomas are a Hollywood couple: an entertainment lawyer and movie star, who also are well-known for their fly fishing exploits. They live in Santa Monica, CA and Wilson, WY

Skip graduated from the US Air Force Academy and received his law degree from UCLA. He is a senior partner of Ziffren, Brittenham, Branca & Fischer, an entertainment law firm which has one of the largest television, music and motion picture practices in the world; it also specializes in entertainment mergers and acquisitions. Skip represents a number of major Hollywood stars as well as currently serves on the board of or is a trustee of numerous charitable organizations including Conservation International, The American Oceans Campaign, The Environmental Media Association, and The Alternative Medical AIDS Foundation. He also was a member of the U.S. team in the World Fly Fishing Championship.

Heather Thomas has had the lead role in such feature movies as "Zapped," "Cyclone," "Kiss of the Cobra," "Hidden Obsession," and "Red Blooded American Girl." as well as the lead in numerous mini-series and movies of the week. She has been a television series regular on "The Fall Guy"(ABC) and "Talking with a Giant" (NBC) along with several others. She has hosted a wide range of TV specials from "Miss Teen USA" and "David Copperfield" to guest hosting "American Sportsman." She has appeared on "The Tonight Show," "David Letterman," "Dick Cavett," "Oprah Winfrey," "Live with Regis & Kathy Lee," "Goodmorning LA," and "Mike Douglas." Currently Heather is starring in "Howl," a discussion show for teenagers; and she has two feature film scripts in development. She has fished for ten years from Alaska to Wyoming, Africa to Canada; she was the only woman on the winning One-Fly team in 1991.

Heather and Skip are co-owners of the Firehole Ranch on Lake Hebgen in West Yellowstone.

Heather Thomas, before she'd consent to give me her recipe or biographies for Skip and herself, wanted me to understand two important facts about them, right up front: Skip is a very good fisherman, but no cook; and they both practice catch-and-release religiously...but have had to very occasionally kill a fish.

I would guess that all of the fishermen in this book are ethically bound to the practice of catch-and-release; but too, know there are reasons sometimes to kill fish. We all can recall times when we realize the fish hasn't withstood the fight well and should be saved from a drawn-out death; sometimes we may even choose to succumb to the seduction of the fish's delicate flavor. Heather killed a steelhead for neither of these two reasons. All I can say is that there is somewhere in fish heaven a steelhead who now believes he should have feared the wrath of a woman.

She and Skip were up steelhead fishing with their well-known fishing celebrity friends, the Teenys, on a private river in the Northwest. The stream moved quickly through close woods with trees growing out of the shore. There were big holes in the water so it was hard to fish in the stream without going in over your waders in spots, and hard to cast from the shore and not get entangled. Donna Teeny was showing Heather how to do that big, long roll cast that lessens the tree entanglement problem. Heather must have been getting the hang of it pretty well because she suddenly hooked into a huge steelhead who decided to take leave and head at breakneck speed down stream, taking as much line as possible with him. It was hard to keep up, Heather couldn't play him from the stream and she didn't want to horse him in and risk losing him either, so she began "running" along the wooded shore, passing her rod from hand-to-hand around the trees. The rough-barked tree as well as the flying spin of the reel handle managed to beat up her knuckles so badly that by the time the fish was landed her hands were a bloody mess. Imagine her delight when she found that this perpetrator of pain had a slashed fin. The very slight sense of remorse at wanting to end the thuggy fish's life disappeared when she realized it wasn't a wild fish; this "kick-butt" fish was now doomed to be dinner.

Although a somewhat unconventional reason to not catch and release, it probably was not so bad for the fish: dragging a true American beauty down a stream and then ending his days basking in her apple and sweet onion marinade. Actually, I'd say for a fish it's not a half-bad way to go at all.

GRILLED STEELHEAD WITH APPLES,
SWEET ONIONS AND SAGE

6 steelhead (or salmon) steaks about 8 ounces each
2 cups unsweetened apple juice
1 large Vidalia onion or other sweet onion, cut into ½" slices
2 cups peeled and sliced tart green apples
6 garlic cloves, crushed
2 tablespoons soy sauce
5 sprigs fresh sage, plus several for garnish
¼ cup olive oil
Salt and pepper

In a large, shallow baking dish place the steelhead steaks, apple juice, onion, apple, garlic, soy sauce and five sprigs of sage and cover. Refrigerate for six to eight hours or overnight. Remove fish from the marinade and blot dry; reserve the marinade. Fashion a fish grill from branches of olive, apple or cedar and tie the steaks on top (or use a wire fish grill).

When coals are glowing and ash covered, add soaked dried rosemary branches, if available. Grill the fish, basting frequently with olive oil, for 10 minutes per inch of thickness (measured at thickest point), until it is just barely opaque and flaky.

While the fish is grilling remove the sage leaves and garlic from the marinade and discard. Scoop out the apples and onions with a slotted spoon and sauté together in 2 tablespoons of the olive oil for two to three minutes. Add 1 cup of the marinade and bring to a boil and season with salt and pepper. Arrange fish on a warm platter and spoon sauce over top, garnish with sage.

SIG BUCHMAYR

Sig Buchmayr started his career in the outdoor field selling advertising first for *Field & Stream* and then for *Camping Journal*; while his brother, Norbert, sold advertising for *Outdoor Life*. In 1975 the two brothers started their own publishers' representative firm; initially selling advertising for such magazines as *Fly Fisherman Magazine*, *Backpacker*, *Camping Journal*, *Alaska Magazine*, and *Gray's Sporting Journal*. Today, Sig represents *Ducks Unlimited Magazine*, *North American Hunter*, *Guns*, and *American Handgunner*; also, a trade publication called *Shooting Industry*.

Sig grew up in Manchester, Vermont, the first of triplet sons (and namesake) born to the famous Austrian ski meister, Sig Buchmayr. Father Sig came to the U.S. in the early 1920s and started the first organized ski school in America in Franconia, New Hampshire. Sig and his brothers lived near Lye Brook and the famous Battenkill and in the late 1950s and 1960s were usually the only fly fishermen on the two streams. They also were the first to hunt seriously for partridge in the now well-known area of Dorset, Vermont.

Although Sig has maintained a home in Dorset since 1976, he also resides in Connecticut, not far from Long Island Sound and near where he can fly fish for striped bass and bluefish. Stripers and bluefish became as much a passion for the Buchmayr brothers as trout and partridge, and they hosted many fishing expeditions to Nantucket Island for stripers and blues. In 1981 Sig's brother, Norbert, was killed in a car accident just before the annual trip.

At the age of 45, Sig married for the first time. He and his wife, Renee, now have two sons, Brandon and Trevor. Family vacations are spent on Maui windsurfing and traveling out West to snowboard.

Sig Buchmayr and, to a certain extent his brother, Norbert, taught me about an important element in hunting and fishing: Camaraderie.

Camaraderie, for some reason or other has a male connotation. I guess because it is men who are comrades, not women — unless we're talking in a communist state. Women have friends and pals, but not comrades. And it was Norbert Buchmayr who was such a genius at inspiring the true male kind of camaraderie.

Perhaps with their European upbringing (Austrian and British) the Buchmayrs fell naturally into bringing to the outdoor publishing world the concept of house parties, long three or four day parties that included sporting events as well as drinking and eating and general merry-making. Sig and Norb used to host several of these house party weekends for clients (advertisers), ad agency people, publishers and friends. Some were in Dorset, Vermont, at Sig's house, for partridge and woodcock hunts and late in the year, weekends for deer hunting. And Norbert would host a granddaddy of a house party for a week in Nantucket for bluefish and stripers. This was an all-male event (camaraderie, remember) so it was a bit tricky to figure out what to do with me, since I was a publisher and fisherman. The solution seemed to be to have Ed and me rent a house nearby and join into the festivities at opportune moments, such as mealtimes. But I was determined to learn to surfcast and tried to spend as much time out on the beach as possible. I ran into Norbert out on Great Point. He had been up all night, not so much because the fishing had been good, but because he'd driven the hour on the sand out to Great Point and then ran out of gas. That wasn't so bad until he "borrowed" a can of what he thought was gas from the back of some jeep and then found to his dismay he'd poured water into the gas tank. "Hell with it, I'll stay out here and teach her to fish."

"Two hands, all the way back, don't open the bail, lower hand pushes down hard on the bottom part of the rod, throw it long. You're missing where the fish are!" Norb yelled. My arm, my shoulders, everything hurt. The crease in the joint of my index finger was bleeding from the monofilament twanging out of its hold. Norb went to deal with the car. I stayed trying to pull myself together for one or two more casts. Norb returned. "Not many wives come surf fishing with their husbands. You like this?" he said, looking completely puzzled. I was trying to remain standing as the surf pushed me over. "It's sort of a pain-pleasure thing, I guess." I smiled meekly.

Later I walked up the driveway of Westy's house, where the men were staying. I found Norbert lying spread-eagled on his back in the middle of the driveway, still wearing his waders and fast asleep. I stood over him watching him snore on the tarmac. "Did you catch one?" he said with his eyes still closed. "No, but I'll bet I can cook one." Norb laughed and jumped up and grabbed the beautiful striped bass that was lying on the grass. He scaled and gutted it and then "steaked" it, left the skin on and cut through the backbone to the belly. I cooked it perfectly and we all ate it and it was divine. It was the last time we caught big bass for many years. It was also the first and last time I fished with Norbert before he was killed.

Where Norb's house parties were rough and scruffy, all-male debaucheries; Sig's weekends were couples, men bird hunting, ladies antiquing . . . or hunting if they chose to; saunas and fires in the fireplace of the restored Vermont farmhouse; still a bit of debauchery but much more refined. The food seemed always to appear as if by magic, some current girlfriend or sister-in-law had sent it or Sig had some adept male cook come for the weekend specifically to prepare meals so the female guests wouldn't have to.

And then in more recent years, Sig has co-hosted a huge game dinner at the local inn. Invitations requested the donation of game, but it need not be cooked — the chef at the inn would prepare it. The burden of preparing the food was never left to the women, unless they wanted it that way, as upon occasion I would. Then I would slip into the kitchen to kibitz on the sauce or confer on how long to cook the partridge. Sig would often be there, hovering, making sure all was well, drinks were freshened, and talk, sometimes important talk, sometimes jokes . . . would happen while in the kitchen and I would think how nice a weekend of being with friends it was.

Norb was truly a "man's man." And Sig, well, not the exact opposite. But I would call him a "lady's man" in the classic sense (although not so much now that he's a family man) and in a different sense, too. Sig seemed to know how to make the word camaraderie include women . . . and he's one of the very few men who knows how to be a friend to a woman, even if it is still in the kitchen.

This bluefish recipe is a basic standby used by Sig, but was developed by his late brother. Norb really enjoyed cooking and had many recipes for both fish and fowl alike.

BAKED BLUEFISH

2½ pounds bluefish fillets, scaled but with the skin left on
½ cup chopped fresh parsley
⅓ cup chopped fresh chives
3 tablespoons unsalted butter
Ground white pepper to taste
Lemon, cut into wedges
Parsley for garnish
Salt (optional)

Preheat oven to 450°. Use ½ tablespoon of the butter to grease the bottom of an oven-to-table baking dish. A copper-bottomed au gratin pan is ideal. Combine chopped parsley and chives and use half the mixture to evenly cover the bottom of the pan. Place fillets in the pan, skin side down, and cover with the remaining parsley/chive mixture. Dot with the remaining butter and sprinkle with white pepper and a little salt if desired. Baking time varies with the thickness of fillets but should take no longer than 15 to 18 minutes. A toothpick inserted in the thickest part tells the story; fillets are done when no fish adheres. Decorate with parsley sprigs and lemon wedges.

CHRISTOPHER BUCKLEY

Christopher Buckley's most recent novel is *Thank You for Smoking*, which has been translated into five languages and was designated by *The New York Times* as a notable book of the year. He is the author of two other novels, *Wet Work* and *The White Mess*; a play, *Campion*; and a work of non-fiction, *Steaming to Bamboola: The World of a Tramp Freighter*. His journalism and satire have appeared in such publications as *The New Yorker, The New Republic, Vanity Fair*, and *Vogue*. He served as chief speech writer for Vice President Bush and was managing editor of *Esquire*. He is currently the editor of *Forbes FYI*.

Chris Buckley and I have the same kind of relationship that I used to have with my Australian pen-pal when I was eleven: We occasionally correspond, we never talk on the phone, he holds this kind of thrilling mystique for me because his writing is so brilliant and witty, and I've never met him. Well, I may have met him 25 years ago at the twenty-first birthday party of our mutual friend the Russian princess. She wasn't really a princess; but her beauty, inheritance, and father that had actually escaped from the Bolsheviks in 1918 made her as good as one. But of course, that clouded remembrance of a fleeting encounter has made the mystique all the more intense.

And then we have this other mutual friend, P.J. O'Rourke, who definitely equals Chris in his ability to make me laugh. P.J. and I hunt woodcock together every year and I've become moderately familiar with his singular brand of humor. When I asked P.J. for a recipe for this book he said his recipe was very simple, it had only one ingredient: fish, something he was never able to catch. Since I know P.J. and Chris live near each other, I've envisioned them dropping into each others' homes and launching into these riffs of incredible humor; sort of a Seinfeld show intended for WASP, right-wing Republicans, an audience older than twelve . . . and actually funny. I've wondered if they share "material," since the title for Chris's book, *Thank You for Smoking*, sounds so P.J.-esque. But then Chris's recipe arrived — humorous, clever and very good. And I do know with absolute certainty that P.J. had nothing to do with authoring a good recipe. I have been in his kitchen.

CHRISTOPHER BUCKLEY'S SHAD ROE

1. Buy as many sets (two pieces) of shad roe as you can during shad roe season, (February-March).
2. Cook up a lot of thick hickory-cured bacon in a large cast-iron skillet and save the grease. Don't worry about your cholesterol count. Choosing between living forever and eating as much shad roe as you can is a no-brainer.
3. When the bacon is cooked, take it out and set it aside.
4. Clarify some butter
5. Dredge the sets of shad roe in flour mixed with a bit of pepper and paprika.
6. Add some of the clarified butter to the skillet.
7. Heat the skillet to medium-high.
8. When the grease is hot, put the shad roe in the skillet. Cook them until they explode, splattering you painfully with fish egg shrapnel.
9. Remove shad roe, crumble liberally with bacon, and serve with lots of lemon wedges, new red potatoes with dill, bibb lettuce with vinaigrette.
10. Wine recommendation: Sancerre (white Loire Valley wine), or any dry white wine.
11. Lie to the doctor.

STEPHEN BYERS

Stephen Byers was the editor-in-chief of *Outdoor Life* magazine from 1994 to 1996. He writes, "I lost many years to sport on the rivers of Montana and Idaho from which I occasionally wrote feature stories for *Esquire, Outside, GEO, Sporting Classics* and other magazines. I parlayed what I'd learned from that sporting life into the position of editor-in-chief of *Outdoor Life.*"

Along the road to *Outdoor Life*, he held a variety of editorial jobs at Atcom Publishing (their flyfishing and scuba diving magazines), *Mercedes Magazine, Montana Outdoors* and most recently was Senior Features Editor of *Men's Journal*.

Steve Byers' piece for this book came to me differently than any of the others: the fame of his recipe, in fact the recipe itself, preceded him.

Ed and I were having lunch in New York with the editor of *Men's Journal*, John Rasmus, and I asked him if he knew anyone with a good fish recipe who was a fisherman (or maybe it was a good fisherman with a fish recipe?). He responded without hesitation with Steve Byers' name. "And it's for shark." He grinned. Well, of course, it's for shark, I thought. It's from a New York editor, what else would it be for?

I'd never met Steve, but I didn't have any recipes in the book for shark so I went in pursuit, albeit somewhat cautiously (I never have felt it was safe to go back in the water after "Jaws.") I got his recipe fairly quickly and was relieved to find that he listed alternative fish to the shark (tuna and swordfish). But then I really needed his biographical data or how else was I to determine if this was BYERS' SHARK recipe or Byers' tuna with mayo? I spent the next three months trying to get Steve Byers bio. I wrote, I telephoned, I faxed, I became best friends with his assistant, Louisa; and at long last, I began to threaten, nicely. I faxed him that if I were spurned too long I got vindictive. I didn't understand how any man could have a great fish recipe but then have no life, and if he didn't respond to my request I would be forced to make up his life story — or worse yet get his public relations department to dribble something out. This did bring a response, but alas no biographical information. As a last resort I went to New York. My appointment was with Steve...but first I was to see his very nice managing editor. I waited. At long last I met Stephen Byers: flashing eyes, a good grin and a dandy set of suspenders atop a crisp, cool shirt and power tie; I decided he didn't quite strike me as the shark type. No, Steve Byers is brown trout, a brown trout in August, a brown trout in August at mid-day; i.e. a great fish and the master of elusiveness. But then again with some tenacity, we did get him. So who's the shark here?

BYERS' BROWN TROUT SHARK

1 shark steak (or swordfish or tuna), 1½" thick
1 cup homemade mayonnaise (see below)
½ cup fresh squeezed lime juice
¼ cup powdered ginger
Salt and pepper

Salt and pepper the steak and place in a container with a lid. Combine the homemade mayonnaise, lime juice and ginger and pour over the steak. Seal and place in the refrigerator for no longer than 20 minutes, while you get the coals going. Place the grill about 1/16" from very hot coals. Flame the steak, searing it on each side for about three minutes per side, check for doneness (the shark should be slightly blackened on the outside and juicy but flaky on the inside).

FOR HOMEMADE MAYONNAISE:

3 egg yolks
¼ cup vinegar or lemon juice
2 teaspoons prepared mustard
½ teaspoon salt
¼ teaspoon ground pepper
Dash of cayenne pepper
2 cups oil

In a bowl combine the vinegar, salt mustard and both peppers. Let the salt melt. Add egg yolks. Whisk until frothy and well combined. Add oil very slowly in a dribble until the mayonnaise seems to have started to thicken. Then you may add the oil faster. When finished, taste for seasoning and adjust. Whisk in a tablespoon of hot, hot water to finish it off.

SILVIO CALABI

Silvio Calabi is the Editor-in-Chief and General Manager of Down East's Outdoor Group which consists of three publications — *Fly Rod & Reel*, *Fly Tackle Dealer* and *Shooting Sportsman*. In addition to the three magazines, the Outdoor Group sponsors The National Fly Fishing Show and The International Fly Tackle Dealer Show which were both initiated under Silvio's directorship.

Silvio is the Founding Director of the North American Fly Tackle Trade Association. He has authored four books; *The Illustrated Encyclopedia of Fly Fishing*, Henry Holt & Co.; *Trout and Salmon of the World*, Wellfleet Press; *The Collector's Guide to Antique Fishing Tackle*, Wellfleet Press; and *Gamefish of North America*, Wellfleet Press.

Silvio Calabi has always managed to be part of the fortunate group of outdoor magazine editors whose publications were located away from a city . . . far, far away from the city. For an outdoor magazine to be closer to the out-of-doors than to revolving doors is logical certainly, and actually sort of trendy right now. But for many years if you weren't located in Boston, Chicago or New York City, your publishing company was doomed to obscurity and certain failure and you as editor were probably a rather unsophisticated and guileless guy who lived plainly and modestly.

Fly Rod & Reel started in Manchester, Vermont; was purchased by Down East Publishing and moved in the early 1980s to Camden, Maine. Silvio went with it and grew with it so that he now manages a mini-empire of consumer publications, trade magazines as well as shows (trade and consumer), all in the outdoor field — all from Maine. Silvio had grown up in Massachusetts and gone to Middlebury College in Vermont and always stayed pretty much in the rural parts of New England so it's not too surprising that I imagined him as a plaid woolen shirt and pickup truck kind of guy. Wrong. That first time we met he may not have been wearing a tie, but there probably was a classy tweed sports jacket. And I know for certain there was a Maserati, and the next time I saw him a

Porsche, and then there was the $100,000 BMW. Once I think he did get a Range Rover, probably to maintain a modicum of country image. It turned out that this parade of fabulous vehicles was not a result of Silvio having built a publishing empire, except in the sense that his writing now extended beyond fly fishing and Down East; he was writing some sort of column about cars and getting loaners to "test." It was brilliant. He'd chosen the simple life of country work and play, yet wheeled the ultimate driving machines, a luxury usually allotted only to urban rat-raced men. This was some sort of pinnacle in a quality-of-life choice. Although it wasn't long before quality-of-life choices were fashionable and certainly lacked that element of sacrifice that I had come to believe was an unfortunate, but inevitable, side effect. So despite the fact that the bluefish population is in a down cycle right now, and not a fish a lot of people like to eat anyway, and despite the fact that half a cup of mayonnaise is a lot of cholesterol, I'm going to give Silvio the benefit of the doubt. Mr. Cutting-edge Calabi may just be onto a real trend with this recipe. Well, it's a good one anyway.

CALABI BLUEFISH

1 bluefish fillet from a 9" to 10" fish, or 1 steak per person
½ cup mayonnaise
½ cup Grey poupon mustard

Be certain to kill the fish immediately for the best flavor. Gut, and remove the head and gills. Also scrape off any of the black-looking meat. Leave the skin on the fillets and keep ice around the bluefish while it's in the refrigerator. Combine the mustard and mayonnaise and use a knife to frost the fillet with the mixture. Make certain there is about a ¼" layer of the mustard/mayo all over the fillet. Cook the fish on a very hot, closed grill, skin-side down for about 10 minutes or until the layer of mustard/mayo has become blackened. Scrape the blackened sauce off and serve. This recipe is also good for frozen bluefish.

JIMMY CARTER

Jimmy Carter served as the 39th President of the United States from 1977 to 1981.

In his book about his hunting and fishing life, *An Outdoor Journal*, Jimmy Carter says that his dreams have kept him hard at work first to attend the U.S. Naval Academy, to become a submariner, then as an officer in the pioneer nuclear (submarine) program; later to become a successful businessman, the state senator and Georgia governor and then to run and win the election for President of the United States. And since, it has been to build the presidential library and a Center "within which Rosalynn and I could work productively for the rest of our lives.

"And yet, right through these busy years, there has never been any significant amount of time when I stayed away from the natural areas that mean so much to me. During the most critical moments of my life I have been renewed in spirit by the special feelings that come from the solitude and beauty of the out-of-doors."

Jimmy Carter is not the first U.S. President to profess to be a fisherman; as he notes in his book he "shared a love of this art" with George Washington, Chester Arthur, Calvin Coolidge, Herbert Hoover, Dwight Eisenhower, Grover Cleveland...and then George Bush. However, it is sometimes difficult to know exactly how much of a fisherman a famous person really is, particularly a president of the United States.

One of the first streams I ever caught trout from in New England was the Dead Diamond River at the Dartmouth Grant in New Hampshire. I had been frustrated by other streams in the East, finding them relatively sparsely filled with small, difficult-to-catch trout. But we came to the Grant (a true land grant given to Dartmouth College back when the King of England could still do that) with our children because Ed knew it to be the place where anybody could catch fish. And we did. Each day we all caught many brook trout, big and little brook trout. A surprise to me based on my previous experience fishing in the Granite State streams, but not to Ed who knew the story. It seems that in the 1950s President Eisenhower had visited the Dartmouth Grant on a fishing trip. The New Hampshire Fish & Game Department had wanted to ensure that the President of the United States had the best possible fishing and so had stocked the Dead Diamond with a truck load of the brood fish from the hatchery. Mr. Eisenhower had barely wetted his line when he was called away on some national emergency; leaving many great-grandma brook trout to spawn generations of big healthy brook trout for us to catch handily some decades later.

Fishing is such a democratic (and Republican) pastime that it is easy to see why politicians and presidents looking for popular support are eager to project the image of egalitarian fisherman. With over 50 million people licensed to fish, and then more that fish license-free in saltwater, or at very least have a grandfather or son who love the sport; fishing can be appreciated and identified with by most folks, in all parts of the country and from all walks of life. So it is difficult at times to tell if stocking the stream is an attempt to assure that the photo opportunity validates the President's competency and experience as a fisherman no matter what his skill and knowledge really may be; or was it Fish & Games desire to make their state's stream memorable for the leader of the most powerful country in the world?

Certainly President Carter had his share of fishing photo opportunities just as President Eisenhower had endured them before him. It was difficult to know exactly how much of the "real thing" Jimmy Carter was when it came to fishing. Until we happened in the late 1980s to be visiting the office of our friend Hal Miller, at that time the CEO of the Boston-based publishing company, Houghton Mifflin. Hal was an avid fisherman and, too, his career had been fairly brimming with famous people. Hal was not easily impressed by well-known fishermen. But he was impressed with the book Mr. Carter had written about hunting and fishing and a life of loving the outdoors. *An Outdoor Journal* was in the process of finding a publisher and, although Houghton Mifflin did not end up publishing it, it clearly was not due to Hal Miller's lack of believing in it. And rightly so. The book is the voice of the man that talked to us those four years about the hostages in Iran and the peace negotiations between Egypt and Israel and, but now it talks of bass fishing as a boy and learning to fly fish. Of course, a mellowed voice now, but one no less enthusiastic... and certainly the voice of someone who truly loves and understands the world outdoors. I can't say I've ever fished with Mr. Carter, but I know from having read his book and this last line that I would like to: "It is good to realize, that if peace and love can prevail on earth, and if we can teach our children to honor nature's gifts, the joys and beauties of the outdoors will be here forever." His is the voice of a real fisherman.

And this recipe shows some knowledge about how to cook fish; peanut oil *is* the right choice, despite the Carter proclivity for it. It gets the hottest of the vegetable oils and tastes as good as an olive oil. No need to inject the note "or substitute" next to the peanut oil ingredient. Well, then again I guess Mr. Carter still does probably have a bit of the politician in him.

PRESIDENT CARTER'S FRIED FISH RECIPE

1-2 fish fillets (largemouth bass or sunfish)
1-2 cups A-1 or Heinz 57 sauce
2 cups Bisquick or pancake mix
Tabasco to taste
Peanut oil, enough for deep frying

Cut the fish fillets into strips, about the size of French fries. Add Tabasco to the A-1 and marinate the fillets in the sauce for several hours. Shake the marinated fillets in a bag along with the Bisquick. Deep fry in peanut oil (or substitute). Eat hot or cold.

CHRISTIAN V. CHILD

When Chris Child was in college he took a summer job as a fishing guide at Teton Valley Lodge. His experience in Idaho led him to the position of head guide at the Golden Horn Lodge in Alaska where he served for three years in the Bristol Bay Area when there were only a handful of lodges. This led Chris to a long career as a booking agent for sporting travel adventures, first at Frontiers International and then more recently at Pathways International. Chris' career has enabled him to fly fish and shoot in 15 foreign countries on five continents and dozens of islands in between. Upon occasion Chris has utilized his experiences and journalism degree to publish articles in various outdoor publications. Currently Chris is working in real estate marketing and development. He says, "I still love to fish, mostly with the rapier wit Melisse (his wife) on private ponds near my home in Park City, Utah, but in recent years my focus has been on bird shooting, training bird dogs, and snowboarding."

Chris Child (or C.V. as some of us need to call him in order to clarify which Chris of our woodcock hunting friends we're addressing) lived quite near us in New Hampshire for a short while. We used to talk about fishing the upper White together, but never did it. I believe he tried it by himself once and got poison ivy wading wet. Since he's moved back to Utah we only write now about trout fishing and recipes:

"I have made this dish for 17 years but have never thought to write it down. I suspect a lot of fish and game recipes are in people's heads. I learned the technique from Randy Berry and John Pearson, the owners of the Teton Valley Lodge. I got started with them in college when I worked for my college newspaper as a reporter. I saw an ad in that paper's classifieds that said Fly Fishing Guides Wanted. I went to an interview and got a job as a rookie guide for The Teton Valley Lodge, which at the time was the largest fly fishing lodge in the United States. Little did I know what that summer, which was in 1979, would lead to. I guided the south fork of the Snake, Henry's Fork, Fall River and Teton River. The highlight of the season was the upper Teton, which originates in the Teton Valley that surrounds the little town of Driggs on the Idaho side of the Tetons. The river flows right past the lodge and is a slow moving, wide, meandering spring creek that is weedy and full of trout that slurp tiny dry flies. The sports are taken out by the guides in 22-foot Jon boats that each have two swiveling captain's chairs mounted on them. The guides sit in the back of the boat next to the engine and hold the boat in place with poles while the sports cast downstream at feeding trout. As the fly approaches the trout's feeding lane, the sports kick line out of the boat with their rod tips. Usually, right before the fly goes over the trout, the sports call out: "Give'm boat, boy," which prompts the guide to gently release the boat allowing the fly to float freely for a few feet more without any drag. I have not witnessed a slower take. The rule of thumb on the upper Teton is to count to three once the trout has taken the fly before setting the hook. The upper Teton is surrounded by marshes and flat pasture land where cows and sandhill cranes feed along the river bank. At a client's request, we would prepare a Dutch oven shore lunch made from the small trout that were caught down river from the lodge, which was positioned at the headwaters. I don't know but wouldn't be surprised if the lodge no longer puts on those shore lunches because of the fanatical catch-and-release doctrine. In defiance of my strong conservation ethic, I plan at least one trout bagging trip a year and prepare this meal that has delighted hundreds of CEO'ish fishing folk for decades along the Teton River.

"The Teton Valley is the northern-most settlement of the original Mormon colony that by the 1890s spanned the West from southern Idaho to northern Old Mexico. In honor of Teton Valley Lodge owners Randy Berry and John Pearson, who are both devout Mormons and two of the greatest gents I've ever met in the outdoors, I recommend the meal be served with well-chilled soft drinks and a heavy round of chocolate chip cookies for dessert. And as a side dish, double wrap quarter sections of corn-on-the-cob in foil and set them on the coals, turning them every few minutes with a stick so that they don't burn. Start the corn as soon as coals start to form at the edge of the fire."

C.V. is not a Mormon. But from my years of woodcock hunting with him, I can say of him the same as he says of Randy Berry and John Pearson: Chris Child is as fine a gent as I've met in the outdoors. And as far as the soda and chocolate chip cookies are concerned, they'll do just fine. I think the Teton Valley and the amount of pepper in the following recipe would produce enough of a high for me and Chris and probably everyone else on the trip.

TETON TROUT AU POIVRE

10 trout cleaned (8"-10" in size) with heads and tails retained
1 can black ground pepper
2 lemons
1 pound bacon
1 pound butter
Dutch oven
Shovel
Pliers
Spatula

Build a fire using the deadfall from willows that line the stream bank, or from wood split the size of small kindling. Small pieces of wood turn into coals faster, which hastens the cooking process and gets you back on the river quicker. As soon as the fire starts to subside, lower the Dutch oven onto the fire with the pliers and cook the pound of bacon. Don't overcook bacon as it will be finished off when the trout are cooked. When the bacon is done, remove the Dutch oven from the fire and set the cooked bacon aside on a paper plate. Slice lemons into half-circles. Liberally sprinkle each trout with pepper so they are encrusted with pepper. The pepper quantity should be well beyond your comfort level. After pepper is applied, stuff each trout with lemon slices and cooked bacon. Layer the Dutch oven with the stuffed, peppered trout. Add 4 sticks of butter on top of the trout. Cover with heavy lid. With shovel, push the coals of the fire aside making a depression for the Dutch oven. Set the oven over the depression and cover the top of the oven with coals using the shovel. Cook for 10-15 minutes. Depending on how hot the fire and the day is, the trout may be done after 10-15 minutes. If they are not done place the covered Dutch oven back on the fire for 5 minute intervals until the trout are cooked through. The best way to determine if a trout is cooked is to pull on the dorsal fin. If the fin pulls away from the spine of the trout effortlessly, the trout is done. The bottom layer are for the guides to share as those trout will be slightly burned, but also will take on more twang from the pepper and bacon. The butter absorbs some of the pepper flavor leaving a strong but not punishing flavor that is remarkable.

THOMAS AQUINAS DALY

Tom Daly was educated as a graphic artist at the University of Buffalo and then spent 23 years in the commercial printing business before leaving to pursue a painting career in fine art in 1981. Since that time he has been featured in many exhibitions at galleries, museums, and universities throughout the country. President Gerald R. Ford recognized Tom's work by awarding him Grand Central Art Gallery's Gold Medal at the opening of his 1987 show in New York. In addition to his book, Painting Nature's Quiet Places, Tom's work has appeared in numerous publications such as *Gray's Sporting Journal, Sports Afield, Wildlife Art News, American Artists, Sporting Classics*, and *Southwest Art*.

Tom lives on a farm in rural western New York State and paints what he knows: "The landscape of the outdoorsman — whether hunting, fishing, trapping, wood cutting or plowing fields." In winter and when not painting he hand crafts bows, decoys, and fly rods.

Tom Daly went to Alaska with us on our very first GSJ group fishing trip. We took a two-week trip with ten people and fished several different rivers in the Bristol Bay area of Alaska. Tom had been able to join us because we had a guest drop out at the last minute. We thought it could be a nice bonus to substitute with a painter, someone who could "record" the trip in a meaningful way and depart in an instant; so we invited him. We knew his work, he'd been on numerous front covers of *Gray's Sporting Journal* and allowed several of his paintings to illustrate my first two cookbooks. But we didn't really know him, and it could have been a bit risky. We'd heard about eccentric artists who were egotistical and demanding, rude to the other guests, not very good fishermen and did nothing but play the role of prima donna artiste. Tom, of course, turned out to be wonderful; thoughtful, fun, and clearly as astute as his paintings represented — a true addition to the group. He made sketches, photographs and 'quickie' watercolors that he then took home and turned into magnificent little paintings of Alaska.

People who'd been on the trip were to have the opportunity to buy the paintings; Ed and I would get first look at them. We passed the watercolors before us until we both paused for a while at the image of a female nude returning from the familiar bana (steam bath tent) along the banks of the Nushagak. Yes, there had been two other women on the trip, maybe 15 or 20 years my senior, older than the nude as well. My mind searched through the recollections of Alaskan moments, as Ed's eyes searched my face. I did not recall this scene.

We settled on the purchase of a lovely grey-blue watercolor of an Alaskan gravel bar, a lone fisherman seated on a piece of driftwood with arm extended toward the fire. The lunch fish lie on the rocks before him as he pokes straight-armed at the flames with a long stick.

Tom says he paints what he knows. He also professes not to know about cooking which is probably why the man in the picture isn't actually cooking the fish, just poking the fire. He says he leaves the cooking to his wife because she does know it. And the nude? I'm guessing Tom was truly painting what he knows, and with some imaginative importing, did a little pop-on nude of his wife and placed her in the Alaska scene. I'm hoping . . . and grinning.

Chris Daly writes, "I learned a lot of what I know in my Swedish grandmother's kitchen. Standard fare was any conceivable combination of fish and potatoes . . . she had an infinite repertoire. Her food was basic and unpretentious, usually loaded with butter and cream. These are three of Tom's favorites.

POACHED SALMON WITH NEW POTATOES AND EGG SAUCE

1 salmon about 4 to 6 pounds cleaned and gutted
Water (to cover fish)
2 tablespoons lemon juice
2 teaspoons salt
A few peppercorns
2-3 sprigs of parsley
1 bay leaf

In a wide pan combine water, salt, lemon juice, peppercorns, parsley and bay leaf. Bring to a boil and allow to boil for 15 minutes. Add the salmon, cover and gently simmer until done (10 minutes per inch at the thickest part of the fish). Remove skin and bones and break into serving size portions. Drizzle with egg sauce and lots of fresh chopped parsley.

EGG SAUCE

¼ cup butter
1 tablespoon flour
1 cup milk
2 teaspoons prepared mustard
2 hard-boiled eggs
Salt and pepper

Melt butter in a small pan and stir. Gradually add the milk until blended. Stir in mustard, salt and pepper. Continue stirring until thick and bubbly. Gently stir in eggs.

BEER BATTERED WALLEYE

2 walleye fillets
⅔ cup beer
⅓ cup lemon juice
1 egg
½ cup flour, plus flour for dredging
½ biscuit mix

Whisk together the beer, lemon juice, egg, flour, and biscuit mix to make a batter.

Season the dredging flour with salt and pepper and any other herbs you think would be nice and roll the walleye fillets in it and then dip in the batter. Deep fry in oil that has been preheated to 375°, and cook until golden. Drain well and serve.

JOHANNSON'S TEMPTATION

3 onions, sliced into rings
2 tablespoons butter
6 potatoes, julienned into ½" strips
1 2-ounce can anchovies
1 cup heavy cream

Sauté onions in butter until golden brown. In a buttered 2-quart casserole, alternate layers of potatoes, onions and anchovies. Pour cream over all and dot with a little more butter. Bake at 350°, uncovered, until potatoes are tender (45 to 55 minutes).

JACK DENNIS

Jack Dennis' fishing career started at the age of 12 when he sold his first flies. He started guiding anglers at the age of 14 and by 19 he had opened his first fishing tackle business in Jackson, Wyoming. Jack has written several books on fly tying including *Western Trout Fly Tying, Volumes I & II* and his most recently published *Tying Flies with Jack Dennis and Friends*. In addition, he has produced 15 fly fishing video tapes, several of them winning video of the year awards.

As founder of the Wyoming Galleries and the Jack Dennis Outdoor Shops, his clients have included U.S. presidents, movie stars, and sports figures. And Jack has appeared on four ABC television American Sportsmen Shows, ESPN "Fishing the West" and "Fishing North America."

Jack was a member of the Trout Unlimited Team in the first Russia-United States Angling games and was on the U.S. Fly Fishing Team in the World Fly Fishing Championships of 1988 and 1991. He is also one of the founders of the Jackson Hole International One-Fly Competition which, during the ten years since its inception, has raised over $100,000 to save the Snake River cutthroat. He has advised the governments of New Zealand, Australia, Chile, Argentina, and many western states on tourism and fly fishing and helped develop for Frontiers (the largest hunting and fishing travel agency) new and diverse travel destinations. Jack has been a consultant to many manufacturers including Cortland Line, Scott Rod, Abel Reels, Simms, Action Optics, Dan Bailey flies, Griffith Tool, etc.

Jack lectures over 100 days a year. The rest of the time he fishes; as often as possible with his family, including a son and two daughters, and his wife of 25 years, Sandra, an emergency room nurse who shares his love of the outdoors.

Jack Dennis is a man who is very resourceful, but is a bit forgetful. Jack told me that the reason he came up with this dinner all cooked in foil was because as a guide on the Snake River one time he'd forgotten the fry pan at home. When the moment came to cook the streamside meal for his clients he found himself staring into the cooler at a bunch of bowls covered with foil — and nothing to cook the fish or potatoes in. But necessity breeds invention and the idea light bulb switched on; he managed to cook the entire meal in foil. Then finding this eliminated the washing of dishes as well as tasting great, Jack made it a standard method for cooking his streamside meals.

Jack mentioned that the Green Goddess salad dressing substitute in the trout recipe developed out of "another" forgetful guiding experience — this was some other guide's story, of course. I'm not quite sure how Jack got a hold of it. This time the guide forgot bacon and butter and stared into a cooler full of only salad makings. Fearing the fish would stick to the foil without some sort of oil, he tossed on the salad dressing. The trout was delicious.

Jack stopped cooking on open fires in 1973 when the ban along the Snake went into effect. He then started to cook his foiled dinners on a Kangaroo Kitchen, a self-contained propane cooking unit. And now, with catch-and-release so very important out West, he doesn't keep fish to cook for streamside meals any more.

But if I were to fish with Jack some place in the far wilderness where fish are plentiful and brought from-home-supplies scarce, where an open fire and just-caught fish are essential to the trip; I'd try to induce some forgetfulness from Jack. Who knows what kind of wonder meal we'd get!

JACK DENNIS' NOT-FOILED-FOR-LONG DINNER

1 walleye or nice size trout, cleaned but with head and tail left on
1 pound bacon
1 lemon, cut into wedges
3 tablespoons butter
Salt and pepper
1 can Boston baked beans
1 can Campbell's baked beans
4 tablespoons sweet pickle relish
1 box Oneida Tatter Tots
1 bottle Green Goddess salad dressing

Into the cavity of the fish, put the lemon, butter and a couple of slices of bacon. .Also place a slice of bacon along the flanks of the fish. (Or substitute the butter and bacon by pouring a generous amount of Green Goddess salad dressing inside the cavity and covering the fish. Wrap the fish in double layers of aluminum foil. Make a boat out of aluminum foil and pour the two cans of beans and the relish, fold sides together and double wrap. Place Tatter Tots on a sheet of aluminum foil, cover with second sheet of foil and crimp edges together, wrap again in foil. Throw the potatoes and beans onto the fire for about 20 minutes. The fish will take about a total of 10 minutes to cook and should be flipped at the halfway point. Serve and throw away the cooking pans.

DAVE AND KIM EGDORF

Dave and Kim Egdorf are a husband and wife team who, for 15 years, have owned and operated a sportfishing camp on the Nushagak River in the Bristol Bay region of Alaska.

Dave grew up on a farm in Minnesota; after college he went into the military where he served as a medic. Upon completion of military service, he moved to Denver, Colorado and began a career in aviation. Armed with his commercial pilot's license, he took a job flying air taxi in Dillingham, Alaska in 1978. After several years flying for local lodges, Dave decided to start his own business and in the fall of 1981, he began Western Alaska Sportfishing.

Kim grew up in Idaho where she worked as a hairdresser before realizing there was "life after hair." She decided to take a job at a fishing lodge in Alaska, where she met and married Dave.

Kim and Dave have one daughter and spend their winter months in Hardin, Montana.

K im and Dave Egdorf have been our hosts in rainbow trout camp several times, but the first time we went to their camp in Alaska we had the luxury of a couple of days alone with just them and no other guests. Dave and Ed had flown the last two departing guests into Dillingham and were to pick up supplies for the next couple of days. Kim and I lolled around camp for the few hours they were to be gone. We talked a lot about cooking, what it was like to cook every day for a camp full of fisherman, what problems were unique to cooking in the bush, what were some of her fish recipes.

The conversation was fun, but the two hours the men were supposed to be gone were stretching to three. Kim wanted to get dinner cooking but needed the groceries that were coming to do so. The frequency with which we heard mirage engine noises increased, always dashing expectations, until at long last Dave's Beaver could truly be recognized. The tardiness excuses were made and we waited for the supplies to be brought in. It was quite late even though Alaska's long daylight hours made it seem less so. "What! No groceries?" There was a quiet "discussion" between Kim and Dave. "I gave you a grocery list!" "No you did not!" It, of course, didn't really matter who gave what to whom, or who had lost what; the deed was done. We were now faced with nothing to eat for dinner and the nearest restaurant or grocery store hundreds of miles away. Ah, but we had a river full of fish lying before us. We were obliged with a wonderful pike.

(I am happy to report, and of special note for all wives, that when I was fishing with Dave the next day he was searching in his pockets for a twist-on and found the slip of paper he had so heartily denied having the evening before. Of course, Dave, as the catching fisherman of dinner, was totally absolved.) Kim made Pike Puffs, her own great tempura-like concoction that became nearly my favorite fish recipe that she does. Dinner was spectacular and I came to believe that necessity is the mother of invention. Indeed, it is also the mother of some terrific meals. And later I was to discover from Kim how necessity was the mother of Pike Puff's invention in more than in one instance. Kim writes:

"Since many of our clients love fresh fish, I had to have good recipes. The most popular of which became Pike Puffs (rainbows were, of course, only catch-and-release). The development of this recipe grew out of necessity. I had, with all supplies being flown in and with the nearest store 120 miles away, learned to get along without. Or use my imagination and substitute, one thing there was always a lot of was Krusteaz Pancake Mix and beer. With having to bake 14 loaves of bread a day, I often got caught without flour. That's where the good ol' Krusteaz Mix came in handy. I'd actually heard about beer batter deep fat frying, but had no recipe so it was a lot of trial and error. I had to experiment with the batter because it could get too thick and the Pike Puffs too heavy. Also, deep fat frying was not as easy as I thought. If each chunk of fish wasn't patted dry, the batter wouldn't stick, making a huge mess. The guides would bring me fresh pike (ugly to look at) completely boned. That was trick in itself, and then I would take it from there."

KIM'S PIKE PUFFS

2 pike fillets
2 cups Krusteaz Pancake Mix (it must be Krusteaz)
1 can beer
Enough oil for deep fat frying (2"-3" at least)
2 cups mayonnaise
1 cup sweet pickle relish

Heat the oil very hot. Cut the pike fillets into small chunks and pat dry (don't let the chunks get too big). Combine the beer and pancake mix making sure it doesn't get too thick. Dip each chunk of pike in the batter and then deep fry in oil until golden brown. For an easy dip combine the mayonnaise and sweet pickle relish. Serve.

DOLLY VARDEN PARMESAN

4 Dolly Varden fillets
4 tablespoons butter
1 cup tomato sauce
1 cup Parmesan cheese (approximately)
Lemon pepper

Preheat oven on broil. Dot the fillets with pats of butter and sprinkle with lemon pepper. Broil in the oven for about 3 minutes. Pour on the tomato sauce and sprinkle each fillet with the parmesan. Return the fish to the broiler until the Dolly Varden flakes easily and the parmesan is golden. Serve immediately.

MICHAEL AND CHRISTINE FONG

Michael and Christine Fong are an outdoor writer/photographers team. Their work has been published in every national outdoor magazine that reports on fishing; and their writing and photos have also appeared in many books. They have fished extensively throughout North America, in Central America, South America, New Zealand, the Bahamas and in Europe. Mike and Chris can be seen regularly on syndicated TV channels in segments of "Charles West Outdoor Gazette" and on ESPN in "Charles West's Backcountry." Michael is a contributing editor to *Fly Fisherman Magazine*. They have been featured with the International Sportsmens' Exposition since its inception. Michael is a promotion specialist for Fenwick and Umpqua Feather Merchants which sponsor the Fongs' speaking engagements across the nation.

In 1992 Michael and Christine also started producing "The Inside Angler"; a discriminating bi-monthly newsletter which reports on and evaluates fishing destinations in western North America, from Alaska to Mexico.

Mike and Chris Fong gave me one of my most memorable food experiences.

We'd known them only through the photographs they'd published in *Gray's Sporting Journal* until we happened to be in San Francisco on a business trip. It was my first time to San Francisco and the work had been at a trade show that precluded anything other than standing under harsh exhibit hall lights for 12 to 14 hours coupled with a diet of ring-dings, fried dough and soda pop. It was the last evening of the show and we were flying home the following day when Chris and Mike, who'd also been at the show, asked if we might want to have breakfast with them before we left. Breakfast was to be in Chinatown. San Francisco's Chinatown is, of course, famous food-wise and the locale in itself was inviting; but then to have the benefit and knowledge of an insider such as Michael for a guide, was a not-to-be missed opportunity.

We'd parked far away and had to walk up and down and through the most amazing series of streets. From sidewalks that passed by big department store windows filled with pretty furniture and mannequins modeling suits, past buildings of the every-city type and those that were San Francisco landmarks; to where it all began to shift becoming the compact, noisy, congested streets of Chinatown. It was like an aberration in process, a whole new world; different alphabet, different voices, different smells, different faces. I was instantly a foreigner and thrust into my tourist mode of frantically trying to assimilate it all — there was so much, I was losing the battle. We were walking too fast, I wanted to dilly-dally awhile and slowly savor every bit of what was going on around me. But then again, I was hungry.

The restaurant was a large high-ceilinged room that could have fit into it four of the tiny tea or poultry shops we'd just passed. Lots of straight-backed chairs and Formica-covered tables, the place reminded me of an old Hayes & Bickfords or a cafeteria without the tray-line. It was crowded, but we found a table.

Instead of waitresses scurrying to and from the kitchen, there was wait staff that came right to the table pushing a three-tiered dolly loaded with food. Talk was unnecessary (good thing because my Chinese was a bit rusty), all you had to do was point at what you thought looked good, and it was yours. No coffee or donuts or scrambled eggs here, in fact the food was only very vaguely recognizable, and then not necessarily as food. For example, there were several webbed duck feet standing on plates; I hadn't realized you could eat those, particularly without the duck body. But I let Michael and Chris guide me in my choices and it was a thoroughly delightful meal. The curious part came at the end of the meal when the bill was to be tallied. Without menus or a chalkboard listing the items or their prices, I wondered how the check was calculated. Surely it must take a genius with a photographic memory to calculate the sum of all we'd eaten. But it was so simple, each empty dish on the table had a fixed price based on its color and size, just count the empty dishes of similar size and color and multiply by the price. A very clever and very different way of managing, I thought.

Actually, I concluded that a different approach to the same problem is often the oriental way. This is certainly true in Chinese cooking . . . and in the recipes that Chris sent me. Yes, her catfish recipe could be just another poached fish, but look again.

STEAMED CATFISH WITH BLACK BEAN SAUCE

4 catfish fillets
¼ cup salted black beans, rinsed
2 teaspoons fresh, grated ginger
1 garlic clove, chopped
2 tablespoons vegetable oil
2 julienned green onions

Place fillets in a heat proof dish that is also a steamer. Prepare a paste by mortaring the rinsed black beans with the vegetable oil. Add the ginger and garlic clove and when thoroughly mashed and mixed apply the paste to the catfish fillets. Steam the catfish for 20 to 30 minutes, depending on the thickness of the fillets. In the last 5 minutes of the cooking, add the green onions.

CURRIED CRAB WITH SHERRY AND GINGER

2 live Dungeness crabs
2 tablespoons vegetable or olive oil
2 bay leaves
½ cup Spanish fino sherry
1 tablespoon chopped parsley
2 teaspoons fresh, grated ginger
2 teaspoons curry powder
½ cup chicken stock

Immerse the crabs in a large pot of boiling water. Cook for 5 minutes after the water begins to boil again. Remove immediately and rinse in cold water. Chill by placing in a bowl with ice cubes. Clean and crack the legs and claws and quarter the bodies. Heat the oil in a large skillet with high sides. Add the crab and bay leaves and sauté over medium heat for 10 minutes. Add sherry and reduce until 2 tablespoons of liquid remain. Remove the crab to a warm serving platter. Deglaze the pan with the chicken stock. Add the ginger, curry powder, and parsley. Pour over the crab and serve with chilled fino sherry and sour dough French bread.

NORTH COAST BOUILLABAISSE

For the stock:

1½ pounds of fish trimmings (head, tail, backbone, etc.)

6 tablespoons vegetable or olive oil

1 cup chopped onions

½ cup chopped carrots

1 cup chopped celery

4 cloves

8 white peppercorns

1 cup dry white wine

4 sprigs parsley

2 sprigs thyme

1 bay leaf

2½ quarts water

Heat the oil in a stock pot and add the onions, carrots and celery and sauté until tender. add all the remaining ingredients and simmer for 20 minutes. Remove and then strain.

Remaining Bouillabaisse ingredients:

½ cup chopped onions

2 crushed bay leaves

½ teaspoon thyme

¼ cup chopped parsley

2 garlic cloves, chopped

¼ cup olive oil

4 leeks, julienned, white part only

5 medium-size tomatoes, chopped

3 tablespoons tomato paste

1 teaspoon saffron

Salt and pepper to taste

20 well-scrubbed clams

2 pounds boned salmon or other firm meat fish cut into 1½"
   chunks

1 pound abalone cut into 1" cubes

1 pound mushrooms (your choice of type)

Heat the oil in a heavy pot and add the onions, bay leaves, thyme, parsley, garlic, leeks tomatoes, tomato paste, saffron and salt and pepper. Sauté the vegetables until tender. Pour in the stock and bring to a boil. Now put clams in first, maintain a high heat to keep stock simmering, and cook for 5 minutes. Add the fish, abalone and mushrooms and simmer for 3 more minutes or until the clams have opened and the fish is done. (Crab, shrimp or prawns can also be substituted for the above seafood.)

CHARLES GAINES

Charles Gaines' extensive career as a writer has ranged from authoring novels and non-fiction books, screenplays for both movies and television, and numerous magazine articles. Most notable are his two novels, *Stay Hungry* and *Dangler*; his non-fiction books *Pumping Iron* and *A Family Place*. His screenplays include "Pumping Iron," a feature documentary; and the feature film "Stay Hungry," directed by Bob Rafelson and starring Sally Field, Jeff Bridges, and Arnold Schwarzenegger. He has written numerous scripts for ABC's "American Sportsman" program and appeared as host on two segments. He also produced and directed two films.

Charles' magazine credits include articles in such publications as *Sports Illustrated, Esquire, Playboy, GEO, Outside, Forbes FYI,* and *Gray's Sporting Journal*. He is a Contributing Editor to *Men's Journal*; Editor-at-Large at *Cooking Light*; and Special Correspondent at *Sports Afield*.

His awards include final nominee for National Book Award for fiction; two Cine Golden Eagle Awards and an Emmy for television writing; and the Writer's Guild of America Annual Award nomination for film writing.

Charles founded Pathways International, a sporting travel company and co-founded National Survival Games. He is also a member of the Anglers Club of New York and a founding member of the U.S. Fly Fishing Team.

Charles and his artist wife of 32 years, Patricia, divide their time between homes in Nova Scotia and Alabama.

Charles Gaines is impressive. There is just no other word for it. Not only because of his professional accomplishments, his obvious athleticism and his good looks; he's managed to stay married to a beautiful and accomplished wife and they've produced three talented children. He can flash dance along with the best glitter of Hollywood, but knows the plain, unglamorous commitment of being a good friend and mentor. And the man can cook, too!

I've often cooked with Charles, and we've hunted woodcock together for going on seven seasons now, but our fly fishing expedition for smallmouth bass in Nova Scotia was our first fishing trip together. The lake was deep into the wilderness and we'd started out at dawn. There were four of us; Ed and myself, Charles and a Nova Scotian friend and fishing guide. In Charles' big Suburban we drove long dirt logger roads with many turns, then hiked through woods and along the rocky edge of a near-dried-up smaller lake. The walk over the rocks to the lake was difficult, required concentration and some agility, and took close to an hour. But the trek was definitely worth it. Ed and I each hooked the largest smallmouth bass we'd ever caught. And Charles? I have absolutely no memory of what he caught, all I can recall is his awe-inspiring casting ability. Extremely long, tight loops that placed the fly always in perfect position, gracefully and athletically executed; the technique was quintessential Charles. I had seen good casters before, in fact I live with one. But there was something different about Charles' style. It wasn't just that it was as long and precise as world champion Steve Rajeff's; it had a passion and a drive to it . . . to catch fish. Charles was competing, not with me or Ed or even himself; he was competing with nature. And, of course he would win. He was Charles.

But admiration can be a funny thing; it is essential to a marriage and perhaps also to many friendships. It also can be a horrible barrier to any true familiarity or closeness. That barrier with Charles was about to come down a bit.

The fishing day concluded, we started the walk back and reached the car tired and hungry and ready to return to reality. And that we did quicker than we thought possible; upon reaching the car we found that Charles had left the headlights on and the car battery was dead. We were really too far back in on the dirt roads to walk out, but then we were probably too far back in for any vehicle to pass by in this century. Nobody was too pleased about the situation. We sat for an hour or so hoping for a passerby and wondering what to do and then Ed headed in one direction down the road and our guide friend in the other looking for assistance. Charles and I sat on the tailgate and chatted and laughed. He didn't really seem embarrassed with the fact that he'd done something pretty stupid, and I was happy he was back on earth with me. It was one of the nicest times I've had with Charles, except perhaps when we cook together. There's nothing like good food for a friendship.

NOVA SCOTIA SALMON

1 whole fillet with skin left on (a fillet from a 12-pound fish should
    feed 6 people)
1 cup plain yogurt
4 tablespoons dill (preferably fresh)
2 cups or so of white wine
1 tablespoon rosemary
Juice of one lemon and several lemon slices
Salt and pepper
Fresh dill or parsley sprigs (optional)

When the salmon gets home from the fish market or fishing trip, rinse the fillets in cold water and pat dry. Wrap them individually in waxed paper and store in the refrigerator until ready to cook. First make the sauce by combining yogurt, ground pepper and 2 tablespoons of the dill and let sit in the refrigerator for several hours. Make a large charcoal fire and let it burn down to hot coals or turn on a gas grill to ¾ high. Out of tinfoil make a "boat" and lay the fillet skin-side down in it. Pour the white wine over the fish and add the remaining dill, rosemary, lemon juice, lemon slices, and salt and pepper. The sides of the boat should be high enough to easily come together, crimp them closed. Add a second layer of tinfoil to the boat and place on the grill. Baste the fish with the juices every few minutes. Poach the salmon for approximately 20 minutes and then check for doneness. When cooked the fish should easily pull away from the skin. Remove fish with a spatula to a heated platter and garnish with fresh dill or parsley sprigs. Serve immediately with the dill-yogurt sauce on the side. Or the fillet can then be refrigerated for a nice cold poached salmon lunch.

LARGEMOUTH BASS A LA ALABAMA

4-8 largemouth bass fillets
1 quart vegetable oil (or enough to fill a Dutch oven to a 4" depth)
2-3 cups stone-ground yellow cornmeal
1 tablespoon cayenne pepper
Salt and freshly ground black pepper
1 tablespoon fennel seeds
10 juniper berries
Lemon wedges

Rinse the bass fillets in cold water and pat dry. Wrap in wax paper until ready to cook. Pour the oil into the Dutch oven and begin to heat. With a mortar and pestle grind the fennel and juniper berries together. Add the ground berries and seeds to the cornmeal, cayenne, and salt and black pepper and turn the mixture out onto a piece of wax paper. Dip each fillet in cold water and then dredge in the cornmeal mixture. Let the coated fish sit for 5 minutes and then dredge again in the cornmeal. Refrigerate the bass until the oil has become very hot (at least 375°). Fry the fillets no more than two at a time for about 3 to 6 minutes each. Cut in half to check for doneness. Drain the fillets on a brown paper bag then serve immediately with lemon wedges.

DAN GERBER

Dan Gerber has written articles or poetry for "nearly every magazine" including: *New York, Sports Illustrated, Playboy, New Yorker, Outside, Gray's Sporting Journal, Nation, Partisan Review,* and *Stony Brook* to name but a few. He is also a contributing editor for *Sports Afield.*

Dan originally was a race car driver; driving Shelby-Cobras and 350 GTs in the Pan and TransAms for five years until, as he says, he "set the world's record for deceleration, 110 mph to 0 mph in one second." He crashed into a concrete wall and had to spend the next year of his life getting pieced back together. He says he then became a used car salesman. Dan taught high school English and then English and American Literature at several Michigan colleges becoming writer-in-residence in 1970 at Michigan State University. In 1971 he published his first book of poetry, *The Revenant,* and in 1973 his first novel, *American Atlas.* Since then he has written *Out of Control* (novel) and *Indy: The World's Fastest Carnival Ride* (non-fiction).

Dan Gerber was born on a Monday and lived 52 years in Michigan before moving permanently in 1992 to Key West, Florida where he now divides his time between "four hours of complete idleness, fishing with his yellow Lab named Willa and whatever else he can fit in."

Dan Gerber was not very forthcoming with information about his life. He's not really a shy person and possesses only the normal amount of modesty; he certainly couldn't be withholding details fearing them tedious — not a man who drove race cars for five years and writes a novel entitled *Out of Control.* I had tried what I was taught in Journalism School, to play dumb and have long pauses of silence when interviewing. This is supposed to make the interviewee feel slightly exasperated and nervous and want to fill in the gaps with honest talk. Well, this didn't really work with Dan. I should have remembered from years ago when I met Dan that he's the kind of guy who reveals himself to a woman over perfectly made Tanqueray martinis, not over the phone. Or perhaps he thought I already knew about him. But gossip of Thailand times was not what I was looking for, and so I went to the best source of exposure there is of a writer: his writings.

I remembered that in all my years of reading Ed Gray's *Gray's Sporting Journal*, one of my very most favorite articles had been written by Dan. It was published in 1978 and was about a trip via Toyota truck Dan and his wife, Virginia, were taking across the Kaisut desert to Lake Rudolph in Africa. It's called "Thanksgiving on the Fourth of July." To synthesize his beautifully and well-crafted article seems unfortunate; but for relevancy here it should suffice to say that his story was about coming upon a primitive tribe of spear-carrying Rendili. Dan and his companions where trying to enjoy a glass of champagne (it was the Fourth of July) while the natives were becoming very restless when no gifts of tobacco could be produced. As Dan watched the spears being unsheathed, he gulped his champagne, shook the glass and remaining ice in nervous gesture, and then placed a piece of ice in the hand of one of the tribesmen. The Rendili had never experienced ice and the native screeches in what he believes to be burning pain. Dan eats an ice cube and the Rendili are aghast at his bravery; and then offers an ice cube to the macho man of the tribe to try. After seconds that are an eternity, the Rendili man, with ice in his mouth for the first time, smiles, and all is well; or at least well enough to let them be on their way.

There is worldliness and bravado, fear and sensitivity to be found here. But certainly to glean a great deal about the character of Dan Gerber would require more; a full reading of this story, and probably the other five he wrote for *Gray's*, too, his poems, several of his books and very definitely a drinking of those Tanqueray martinis.

But really what is most relevant here is to know that Dan embarked on this truly death-defying trip for the purpose of catching fish . . . in Lake Rudolph, specifically tilapia. So here's how to cook it.

TILAPIA

4-6 (1 pound) tilapia fillets (which now are a farmed fish in several U.S. states)
1 cup milk
1 cup Bookbinders bread crumbs (must be Bookbinders)
4 tablespoons butter, or 2 butter and 2 good green olive oil
½ cup Matuks West Indian Hot Sauce
½ mayonnaise

Combine the Matuk's and the mayonnaise to make the sauce. Dip each fillet in milk and then dredge in bread crumbs. Fry in hot, hot butter and serve immediately with the sauce, steamed spinach and red potatoes.

TED AND MARY GERKEN

Ted and Mary Gerken have been co-owners and operated the famed Iliaska Lodge in Iliamna, Alaska since 1977. And they are as well-known for their gourmet food as they are for their long-time fly fishing program at Iliaska. Ted first came to Alaska during his 24-year service in the U.S. Coast Guard. He has two engineering degrees, a commercial pilot's license and is a licensed hunting and fishing guide. Ted has authored two books. The first chronicles the couple's lodge experiences and the second, the interaction between man and bear.

Mary has been an Alaskan since 1950; she was three years old when her family settled on a homestead in Homer. Growing up in the restaurant business, she spent her early adult years as a storekeeper, postmistress, secretary and bookkeeper in remote areas of Kodiak Island. Her recipes have appeared in several publications including the *L.L. Bean Game and Fish Cookbook*. She also co-edited *Alaska Cooking Classics* which included many of her Iliaska recipes.

Ted and Mary Gerken have introduced many fisherman to Alaska, and they know exactly how to do it. My first fishing experience in Alaska was on Iliamna Lake with the Gerkens. And it was their splendid lead which launched me into a lifelong love affair with that spectacular country. The lodge is straightforward, clean, pleasant and warm — the conversation friendly and uncomplicated. There is no need for airs or fanciness. The Gerkens seem to understand the majesty that is Alaska is best left unfiltered and unfettered, to do otherwise would seem silly.

When the day has included a float-plane flight with sightings of fishing grizzly bears, snow-capped mountains diving into the bluest of big lakes, and multiple casts at near elephant size rainbow trout, what should the evening at the lodge bring? The Gerkens know what punctuates that kind of day the best and so they introduce the quiet side of Alaska. That is a beautiful fillet of salmon cooked perfectly (as evidenced by Mary's recipes below) for dinner, a recitation of a Robert Service poem in Ted's expressive and practiced voice, and an after-dinner toast of Yukon Jack . . . " To the day, to Alaska."

If the measure of a great restaurant is predicated on the ideal blending of bread and circus, of food and ambiance, then truly Iliaska Lodge is a great. Now if only the taxi fare was more affordable.

BAKED SALMON IN MUSTARD CRUMB CRUST

2 sockeye salmon fillets, about 1 pound each, skinned and trimmed
⅓ cup white vinegar
¼ cup sugar
⅓ cup Dijon mustard
1 teaspoon dry mustard
1 cup vegetable oil
1 teaspoon thyme
Salt and pepper
2 ½-3 cups fresh bread crumbs

Preheat the oven to 375°. Place the sugar, both mustards and vinegar in a blender and, with the machine running on low, pour the oil in slowly until blended well. Lightly grease a roasting pan and arrange the fillets in it and season with the salt, pepper and thyme. Spread the mustard mixture evenly over the salmon making sure they are covered completely. Press bread crumbs onto the fish and bake approximately 25 to 30 minutes or until the crumb crust is golden and the fish is done.

GRILLED SALMON WITH TOMATO BASIL BUTTER

1 salmon fillet with skin left on one side
½ cup butter (1 stick) softened
1 tablespoon tomato paste
1 clove minced garlic
3 tablespoons fresh basil, chopped

Several hours before dinner whip the butter together in a food processor or blender along with the basil, garlic and tomato paste. Spoon onto a piece of plastic wrap and roll into a log shape and chill in the refrigerator. Season the salmon with salt and pepper and grill on one side for about 25 minutes or until done. Place a pat of the compound butter (or two) on each serving of salmon.

SALMON BALL HORS D'OEUVRE

1 cup canned, smoked or leftover salmon cut into small pieces
8 ounces cream cheese
1 tablespoon lemon juice
1 tablespoon horseradish
2 teaspoons grated onion
Dash of Worcestershire sauce
½ cup of chopped fresh parsley or chopped walnuts

Combine all the ingredients but the parsley together at room temperature and then form into a ball and refrigerate. Roll the ball in parsley or nuts before serving with crackers.

GRAVLAX-CURED SALMON FILLETS

2 pounds fresh salmon fillets
¼ cup salt
½ cup sugar
1 bunch of fresh dill
2 teaspoon white peppercorns, crushed

Scale and debone the salmon, cutting the fish into two parts along the backbone. Do not rinse the fish but wipe it dry with paper towels. Mix the salt and sugar together and rub the fish with the mixture. Also sprinkle the mixture and a third of the dill over the bottom of an earthenware or enamel baking dish. Place one piece of salmon, skin side down, into the dish and sprinkle generously with dill, crushed peppercorns and the sugar/salt mixture. Cover with a second piece of salmon, skin side up. If the pieces do not match in shape, place the thick side to the thin side. Sprinkle the fish with the remaining salt/sugar mixture.

Cover the fish with a sheet of aluminum foil and a light weight such as a cutting board. The fish will "leach out" in about four to five hours. Then pour off the liquid. Keep the gravlax refrigerated for at least 48 hours before serving, turning the fish at least twice during this period. If properly chilled it can keep for two weeks.

To serve, cut into slices removing the skin carefully. Sauté the skin in a bit of butter in a very hot skillet and then roll up and serve with the gravlax as a garnish along with sliced cucumbers, dill and lemon wedges. Serve with gravlax sauce.

GRAVLAX SAUCE

3 tablespoons olive oil
1 tablespoon red wine vinegar
1 tablespoon sugar
⅓ teaspoon salt
2-3 tablespoons prepared mustard
2-3 tablespoons minced dill
Pinch of white pepper

Blend together all the ingredients except the dill. Add the dill, or serve it in a separate bowl.

RICK AND SUSIE GRAETZ

Rick and Susie Beaulaurier Graetz have combined their love of travel, adventure, and photographic skills to produce books on cities, states and foreign countries. Their photography has appeared in works on the West Indies, Europe and Asia. Susie is the editor of the highly successful *Montana Celebrity Cookbook*, the proceeds of which were donated to the Intermountain Children's Home. Rick is the publisher of *Montana* magazine and CEO of American & World Geographic Publishing.

Rick and Susie Beaulaurier Graetz first were introduced to us in the late 1970s when we used to go on house party weekends to Dorset, Vermont and birdhunt, or occasionally fish the Battenkill. Actually, to be more accurate, it was Rick that we met on those wonderful weekends, for Susie always seemed to be back at home in Montana. I erroneously assumed that her absence was due at least in part to her lack of interest in the field sports.

Rick and Susie's professional lives had always seemed the better version of Ed and Becky Gray's. They, too, had a successful magazine; but theirs was in Montana, sold it for a lot of money (Rick's words, not mine) to new owners for whom they could continue to work and travel the world. Other than having a successful magazine, our business dealings had none of those attributes. They even seemed to happily work together, a quality Ed and I possessed but had been told was unique. But for a long time I thought we had an advantage: Ed and I enjoy the outdoors together and I assumed Susie was a home-body. Well, I was wrong. When I telephoned Rick for his recipe for this book he explained that he really wasn't a fisherman — a rock climber, hiker and outdoorsman, yes, but it was Susie who loved to fish...to fly fish even. And to draw the continuing parallel Susie had a cookbook, too, called *Montana Celebrity* which was a collection of favorite recipes from Montana's famous. I asked for a copy and was delighted by the cookbook, but was interested in how few recipes were for fish — and from residents of arguably *the* fishing paradise. Actually this syndrome followed, to some extent, what I had been experiencing with my cookbook.

Some of the well-known people I requested recipes from preferred not to contribute on the grounds that they didn't want to appear unsupportive of catch-and-release. I objected to this if for no other reason than it implies that the people in the book believe in "catch and keep"; to the contrary. I wrote in my *Gray's Fish Cookbook* on this topic: "I think God really wanted us to eat the fish we caught, but He realized there were a bunch of pigs in the crowd, so He invented the sport fisherman: a creature who would find it appealing just to catch the fish and who would figure out a lot of reasons why we all should put the fish back and not eat it." Twelve years later I explain that a bit more fully by saying that He has created the sport fisherman to actually think about what he is doing, to "catch and regard." Those of us who fish with any regularity will always have reasons to keep and eat the fish as well as reasons to release the fish. We may even hope the reasons for releasing the fish are more prevalent, for fewer fish on the table only enhances the meaning, value, and preciousness of those we must keep.

Susie Beaulaurier Graetz says of her cookbook, "Each recipe is a gift." That is true with the recipes in this book as well. But here our gifts are multiplied times two because every recipe contains the gift of the main ingredient. And I do thank God for really wanting us to eat the fish we catch.

MONTANA GRILLED TROUT

4 whole trout or fillets
1 cup mayonnaise
2 tablespoons prepared mustard
2 eggs
½ lemon, squeezed
½ cube butter
1½ tablespoons grated onion
1 or 2 garlic cloves, pressed
Salt and pepper

Whisk mayonnaise, mustard, and eggs together. Slowly add lemon juice and butter. Mix well and then add the onion and garlic. The batter should be fairly thick. Season the trout according to taste with salt and pepper. Dip the fish in the batter and put on a greased barbecue grill over medium hot coals. Use a spatula to turn the fish half way through cooking. The fish tend to cook quickly, so keep your eye on them. When the fish flakes with a fork, it's time to eat. Pour yourself a glass of good wine and enjoy.

GRITS GRESHAM

Grits Gresham has been a freelance photo-journalist for over 40 years. His work has appeared in *Sports Illustrated, True, Argosy, Gentleman's Quarterly* and in most outdoor, shooting and fishing publications. He is editor of *Louisiana Conservationist* and has been the Shooting Editor for *Sports Afield* magazine since 1974. Grits has also been the Outdoor Editor for the *Shreveport Times* and had a syndicated newspaper column for 20 years.

Grits has authored seven books including *Fishes and Fishing in Louisiana; The Sportsman and His Family Outdoors; The Complete Book of Bass Fishing; Grits on Guns* and *Weatherby: The Man, The Gun, The Legend* which he co-authored with his son, Tom.

Grits currently hosts the ESPN TV show "The Shooting Sports . . . America" and was field host, producer and consultant for ABC's "The American Sportsman" for 13 years. He also hosted and was associate producer of the syndicated series "Sports Afield" for four years and has been the host for numerous TV films, including many for the National Shooting Sports Foundation. For 20 years Grits represented the Miller Brewing Company in their commercials.

He was educated at the University of North Carolina, Vanderbilt, Yale, and Louisiana State University receiving degrees in Forestry and Wildlife Management. He lives with his wife, Mary an artist who collaborates with him in both writing and photography.

Grits and Mary Gresham are a couple I've only spent a modest amount of time with and unfortunately, it was not fishing. But I believe that the Greshams are pretty straightforward folks, and that what you see is exactly what you get.

Ed and I got acquainted with Grits and Mary when the four of us were invited, as part of a group of journalists, on a trip to the British Isles. The invitation was issued from the Barbour Company (those makers of waxed cotton rain gear, Wellingtons and other very British stuff) to editors from the outdoor and fashion publications, strange bedfellows though they be.

We all were to spend nearly a week junketing about London and northern England and then to attend the Jackie Stewart Celebrity Challenge at Gleneagles, Scotland.

The Gleneagles' setting is nothing short of astounding: An extremely elegant hotel built in the 19th century by railroad barons; the food, the service, the amenities are nothing short of exquisite. It is surrounded by massive gardens that accent the drama of the Scottish moors and the whole scene reminds one of something out of an Emma Thompson movie. But with its location not far from the great salmon river Tay, along with the hotel's own sporting courses, the place becomes truly distinctive for me. Famous, of course, are the Gleneagles' golf courses where the Scottish Open has been held several times; there is the Mark Phillips (Princess Anne's ex) Equestrian Center; and then the Jackie Stewart Shooting School and the "Challenges," all at Gleneagles.

The "Challenge" is actual a complicated and intricate sporting clays shooting contest and the celebrities are mostly royals, athletes (like cricket players), movie stars, opera singers; usually British but a few from other European-type countries. Most are unknown to Americans unless they've been involved in a particularly juicy divorce or been satirized by "Monty Python."

But just down the hallway from Ed's and my room was Princess Anne and her entourage of assistants, personal secretaries and bomb-sniffing guard dogs. Dinner included sword-dancing, the haggis and ever-flowing 30-year old single malt scotch. And at the Competition the following day was luncheon with the Rt. Honorable Earl of Litchfield seated to my left (with Mary Gresham to his left). Well, I tried to be witty, vivacious and at least to pretend social quality. Of course, to accomplish that I probably never should have stayed up all night dancing with the swords and the single-malt .

Mary and Grits were what they were. Grits wore his famous hat, shot blisteringly well the morning we were allowed to shoot at the School (and could clearly have out-shot 95% of the competitors at the Challenge), and Mary chit-chatted with the Earl about how the funny British money was hard for her to understand or believe was actually money. That's why she was spending so much of it! I think ol' Litchfield thought she was terrific. And she was.

I was smitten a bit (well, a lot) with Gleneagles, but Grits and Mary seemed to take it all in stride, not ungrateful or shy, just comfortably cruising along and only moderately impressed. They were perhaps more sophisticated than I. Or, they more innately felt the American advantage:

One of the greatest aspects of our hunting and fishing is it's very democratic, and can afford to be because fish and game is plentiful by comparison. English shooting and angling is elegant; but very exclusive, very confined, and restricted to the privileged few. Even as guests in the country and well-known fishermen in our own right, we, Americans were excluded from actually fishing the Tay.

I should have guessed that Grits and Mary would grasp the fatal flaw in British angling and shooting; after all Grits was a man who for 20 years had been saying on behalf of Miller Brewing Company and Miller Light Beer "Great taste, less filling!" I think we'd all agree with Grits; the Brits have great taste, but their fishing sure was less fulfilling.

"There are as many recipes for hush puppies as for cooking fish, and they vary from excellent to awful. Here is my wife, Mary's recipe, which is excellent:"

HUSH PUPPIES AND STUFF (MEANING BASS)

2 cups sifted corn meal
½ cup flour
1 egg, beaten
1 cup diced onions
½ teaspoon baking soda
3 teaspoons baking powder
2 teaspoons salt
Bass fillet(s)
Half buttermilk and half beer

Mix the dry ingredients. Stir in the beaten egg. Add the onions to the batter. Mix with equal parts buttermilk and beer until thick. Chop a raw bass fillet up into very fine pieces — almost grated — and add to the hush puppy batter. Drop batter, 1 tablespoon at a time, in deep fat in which fish has been fried.

If I don't add the fish to the batter, I usually cook some of the plain hush puppies along with the fish, dropping them in between the fillets in odd corners of the skillet. In this case you should wait until the fat has cooled a bit as the hush puppies cook more quickly than do the fillets and the smoking hot fat will burn them. When cooking nothing but hush puppies, after the fish are out of the pan, reduce the heat slightly. Keep them turning and don't overcook.

Drain the hush puppies on absorbent paper, just as you do the fish, and cook twice as many as you think you'll need.

TOM GRESHAM

Tom Gresham is the Arms and Ammo Editor of *Sports Afield* magazine. He is also a columnist for *SHOT Business* and a regular contributor to *Rural Sportsman*. In addition, he is currently the host of "Tom Gresham's Gun Talk," a nationally syndicated live, call-in radio program. Tom co-host's the "Chevy Trucks Shooting Sports America" television series on ESPN.

In 1996 Tom was named Shooting Sports Writer of the Year and named one of the "100 Most Important Radio Talk Show Hosts in America."

Previously, Tom has been the Editor of *Alaska* magazine and of *Rifle and Handloader* magazine. He is a technical advisor to the National Rifle Association. Tom has authored three books and co-authored *Weatherby: The Man, The Gun, The Legend*.

In addition to being a certified firearms instructor, Tom is also a licensed private pilot and a certified scuba diver.

Tom Gresham is a very practical man. I didn't know him at all well, having only conversed with him in cocktail party sign-language at noisy trade shows, until we met with him in Anchorage. Ed and I were about to embark on a trip to Bristol Bay for salmon fishing and Tom was then editor of Alaska magazine. We sat in one of my most favorite bars in the world, atop the Captain Cook Hotel, and talked a little about publishing and a lot about fishing and hunting. I had been to Alaska before but primarily to hunt ducks and catch (and release) rainbow trout. But this time there would be salmon; silver salmon as they just come into the river and jump and are so fresh and fun to fly fish for. Tom was thoughtful enough to suggest a few local smokehouses that he knew of for the fish we intended to bring home but wouldn't be freezing. Oh, I wouldn't freeze them, and not because I am against frozen fish.

I explained to Tom that on a trip to the Ungava several years before we were lucky enough to bring home twelve beautiful Atlantic salmon. Obviously recipe versatility was called for with that kind of catch and poaching was one of the necessary and obvious choices. But it was then

I learned that you should always measure your salmon before you keep it because if it's over 24", it's un-poachable. In all of North America (and probably Europe, too) there does not exist a poacher larger than 24"; I know, I've looked. First, I talked to our French-Canadian publisher friend – a great fisherman, and the person who accompanied us to the Ungava. He had gotten his poacher by welding together two stainless steel sausage containers found in a remote meat packing house in Northern Quebec; not too handy for me. I then spoke with my cooking friends who referred me to restaurant supply houses in East Boston, but who also suggested I own a successful restaurant before attempting to purchase anything there as the prices would require that kind of cash flow. No, I never did find a poacher and I was pretty certain that this Alaskan fishing trip was very likely to produce the same large-size and quantity of salmon, a wonderful glut but perplexing problem. The same dilemma about how to poach them; I couldn't bear it.

Tom listened to me intently and courteously. The solution was simple he said, "Poach large-size fish in the dishwasher." Bizarre, I thought, but very practical. And it works. This is how Tom does it.

TOM GRESHAM'S FISH IN A DISHWASHER

4-6 pound whole salmon, gutted and with the head removed
½ cup soy sauce
½ cup of dark brown sugar
1 lemon, sliced

Combine the soy sauce and brown sugar together in a small saucepan and heat, stirring constantly, until the two ingredients are completely incorporated. Place the salmon in a 'boat' made out of tinfoil and pour/paint the sauce over the fish, completely covering it. Add the slices of lemon and seal the foil tightly. Add a second layer of foil, to insure an air-tight, completely waterproof seal around the fish. Place on the top rack of a dishwasher and run through a complete cycle. Remove and unwrap carefully, pour off the soy and brown sugar mixture and retain for sauce. Slice the fish, add freshly ground pepper to each portion and serve with the sauce. (Can also be cooked on a barbecue. Grill fish for 10 minutes per each inch of girth, measured at the fattest part.)

WINSTON GROOM

Winston Groom wrote *Forrest Gump*; it was published in 1986. His two most recent books, published in 1995, are *Gump & Co.* and *Shrouds of Glory: from Atlanta to Nashville-the Last Great Campaign of the Civil War.* In addition, Winston has authored *Gumpisms: the Wit and Wisdom of Forrest Gump; Only; Gone the Sun; Conversations with the Enemy: the Story of P.F.C. Garwood; As Summer Dies;* and *Better Times than These.* Winston appeared for the first time as an outdoor writer in the February 1996 issue of *Sports Afield* with a quail hunting article.

Born in Washington, DC; he grew up in Alabama receiving his AB from the University of Alabama. He worked as a staff writer for the Washington Star after having served as a U.S. Army Captain in the Vietnam War.

Winston Groom is a very gracious person, I think. I've seen him at dinner parties listen patiently and courteously to the over indulged cocktail blabber of some 50-year old female fan; express great consternation on behalf of his wife who must contend with a major move during his absence; and, despite his hectic travel schedule, he apologizes to me for being overdue with his recipe. Even when one of the most ruthless, cold-hearted and thoroughly unpleasant literary critics in the world shreds *Gump & Co.* to tiny pieces, and Winston is given the opportunity on national TV to trash her, he does so with a certain amount of aplomb: "She didn't like *Forrest Gump,* so why would she be given *Gump & Co.* to review?"

Of course, such graciousness is somewhat predictable from the man who creates such amiable stories about gentle folk and their hard but joyous lives; from a man who writes in long, flowing and adjective-loaded sentences. And then Winston is also a Southern gentleman.

So dare I test his graciousness, dare I test this Southerner by contradicting him on what all male Alabamans hold as sacred and gospel truth: The perfect nature of bream? (Or, as they say "brim.") It is my belief that the smallmouth bass − not the bream − is the "strongest small fish around." Winston did give me permission to edit this piece "anyway I want."

Well, why provoke the man. Let him have his he-man bream — and eat it, too.

"Try this recipt (That's how they spell it in Charleston.). Brim. (Also works for crappy, perch, and other of those kind of fish):

"Screw trout. We don't have those kind of fish down here anyhow. Except in restaurants and they were freeze dried. When I was a kid we'd boat up into the 500 miles of delta above Mobile Bay where there was not much except bears and alligators and snakes and fish for brim. Big bull brim.

"You could use the kind of fly rod you'd buy at Wal-mart, if there had been one in those days — just put a big ole popping bug on it and paddle down one of the eight hundred thousand bayous or creeks or rivers there on a misty spring morning when the mist is still lingering over the tannin-black water and when the sun rises over the trees and marsh and there isn't a single sound except an occasional bird doing its thing and you can see down eight or ten feet to a sandy, grassy bottom, you cast out on those lily-ladened waters and in about five seconds you will have hooked the strongest small fish around — a brim.

Just reel it in. (We don't play around down here like tarpon fisherman or something). By the time breakfast rolls around, you'll have a string (or baitbox full).

Recipt is simple:

Scale bream. Clean bream. Marinate bream in sauce (see below). Cook bream on charcoal grill after letting coals get low (about an hour after lighting).

Bream are done when tender with a fork (about 10 minutes a side, depending on grill, how many bream, whether it's 105 degrees out or — 10 — figure it out). Eat brim with fork and sharp knife to avoid bones. Do not try to eat all of brim, about 5 or 6 good size ones a person ought to do. (Bream weigh anything from ¼ to 1 pound.)

Marinade sauce:

Rule one – experiment. What works for me:
Lea & Perkins barbecue sauce
Bunch of fresh squeezed lemons, with rinds
Pickapepper sauce
White wine
Basil, white and black peppers, salt, garlic, thyme, mustard
A cut up onion
Add Tabasco

Marinate all day, then throw away the bream and drink the sauce. (No, just kidding.)

Serve on a large, hot platter with lemon rinds and celery tops as plate dressing. Actually this sauce works on almost all fish because then they do not taste like fish. They taste like steak with little bones in them.

MIKE HAYDEN

Mike Hayden became Governor of Kansas in 1987, leaving the governorship in 1991 when President Bush appointed him Assistant Secretary of Interior for Fish and Wildlife & Parks. Prior to his election as governor, he served as Speaker of Kansas' House of Representatives from 1983 to 1987.

During service in Viet Nam Mike was awarded the Bronze Star for Valor, the Soldier's Medal for Heroism, and the Vietnamese Gallantry Cross. His undergraduate degree is in wildlife conservation and his master's degree is in biology.

Currently, he is president and CEO of the American Sportfishing Association in Washington, DC. (The ASA is a non-profit trade association working to ensure healthy and sustainable fisheries resources and increase sportfishing participation.) In addition to his ASA duties, he is a board member of the Congressional Sportsmen's Foundation, League of Conservation Voters, and North American Wetlands Conservation Council.

Mike Hayden is known to me by "alliance" . . . and the telephone. A fellow-Midwesterner, an avid fisherman, hunter and wild mushroomer, a politically-powerful conservationist who even Ted Williams speaks of with esteem; I have come to know a little something of Mike through his actions and through the quality and similarity of his interests and associations. He is the real thing; a difficult creature to find in the Washington political scene these days, particularly one so effective. Impressive political and military careers secured, his successes now are as President of the ASA — almost weekly. He works to attain sportfish designations and gill net bans in the states surrounding the Gulf of Mexico and now Massachusetts. He has helped to secure the future of two of my favorite fish, redfish and striped bass. He is important, but gives freely of his time whenever I need research data on fish. And he collects cookbooks on fish and game and talks of an ancient lady he knows who has a great recipe for pomegranate jelly! He writes me, "I have been fortunate in my life to have enjoyed blackened cutthroats in the Grand Canyon, brook trout and chanterelles in Maine, lake trout almondine in Manitoba, and fresh mahi-mahi in Biscayne Bay. But in reality, there is nothing better than deep fried crappie fillets and morel mushrooms with wild asparagus which we enjoy every spring in Kansas. Of course, it goes without saying 'that the fresher the fish the better' — and a good bottle of chardonnay will put a smile on the face of even the severest critic." Thoughts from a true connoisseur. And the recipe below? It is clearly from someone who LOVES to fish, and loves to eat every type of fish he catches.

MOCK SHRIMP COCKTAIL

4-6 bluegill (bream, pumpkin seed or shell crackers)
2 quarts boiling water
3 tablespoon "shrimp boil" seasoning (On the East Coast, the brand name for one of the more commonly-used 'shrimp boil' is "Old Bays." It is actually a combination of 11 spices and can be found under other brand names.)
Bibb or Boston lettuce
Bowl of ice
Tabasco sauce or shrimp cocktail

Fillet the bluegills and cut the fillets into strips by cutting in half the long way. Bring the water to a boil and add the 'shrimp boil'. Plunge the fish fillets into the boiling water and let boil for 45 seconds to 1 minute until blanched. Remove and immediately place the strips on ice. Serve the bluegill strips on a bed of lettuce with either Tabasco or shrimp cocktail sauce.

BOB JAMIESON

Bob Jamieson has been an outfitter since 1976. A wildlife biologist by training, he worked in Alberta and British Columbia and as a game warden in Ghana, West Africa where he helped to establish the national park system. As an outfitter he first guided in the Top of the World (B.C.) area for seven years before moving to the Fort Nelson region where he became a partner in Folding Mountain Outfitters. He now operates a 250-head ranch at Ta Ta Creek, British Columbia and BioQuest International, a consulting firm dealing with resource and land use problems.

Bob is vice-president of the Palliser Wilderness Society, a group instrumental in the creation of the Height of the Rockies Wilderness Area, the first Forest Service administrated wilderness area in Canada. He is also past president and founding member of the Wilderness Tourism Council of British Columbia. From 1990 to 1994 he was a member of the British Columbia Round Table on Environment and the Economy. In 1993 and 1994 he was the East Kootenay Coordinator for the East Kootenay Regional Land Use planning process. He is also a member of the provincial Council on Sustainability.

Bob is currently working on a novel about the early West in Alberta and British Columbia.

Bob Jamieson is the real thing. Not that other outfitters I know aren't the real thing; it's just that Bob really doesn't have even a tiny piece of his life that's citified. Yet he's no backwoods hermit-head either; he's here and now and of this world.

His e-mail to me reads, "Let's see, it's been 3 or 4 years since we talked. So in my life since then. . . well, a divorce to start, then a couple of years of digging to get out from under the double mortgage, then I just got clear of the financial muck and the cattle market goes to hell. Ah, life . . . Ah, but things are all right. I have a fantastic relationship with a wonderful lady, along with three teenagers who keep things interesting; along with 250 cows, a dog, a bunch of horses and assorted wildlife. At the moment I have three early calves on the ground, wondering what the hell happened to the nice warm womb . . . I have started a novel on the early West in Alberta and B.C. Hope to breath a little life into the times when the buffalo died and we broke the grass. Other than that, I'm just kinda camping here, staying put for a change after a lifetime of running around like a rabbit with a weasel on its tail."

And a couple weeks later Bob e-mails Ed, "Life these days mostly consists of looking up a cow's ass. Mid-wife, surrogate mother, the joys of ranching that they don't put in the movies. Just split with the best woman I ever spent time with, cattle market means I'm working this year for nothing and I got kicked in the crotch yesterday. Now, for the good news.

"Spring is coming . . . he says, hands together, looking skyward. Geese are back. Am working on a boundary for huge wildlife refuge that the government will announce, we hope, next month. And there are other women in the world. I guess. I hope. Not meant to depress, just reporting.

"Anyway, fish recipes. I'm afraid I'm not much of a 'conni-sewer' when it comes to fish. The best meal I ever had was in Northern Quebec. We were on a four week canoe trip. We stopped to talk to some Crees that were fishing at the outlet of a lake whose name I have long since forgotten."

The man's solace is in nature, quite naturally; and so he isn't depressing. That's the best part of being the real thing. And in Jamieson fashion, the real fashion, this is a connoisseur's lunch.

JAMIESON BROOK TROUT

4 large brook trout, gutted and cut into four quarters each
2 cans mushroom soup

Put the chunks of brook trout in a pot of boiling water. Add the cans of mushroom soup and boil until the bones fall out. Serve on a piece of firewood, with your butt on the Canadian Shield, the lake mid-day shiny and a 'V' of geese sliding south and a distant gray sky.

STEVEN D. LATNER

Steven Latner lives in Toronto but spends the better part of each summer in New Brunswick where he operates the Sevogle Salmon Club and fishes the Sevogle River, a tributary of the northwest Miramichi, high in the wilderness of the headwaters. Steve writes a little about his background:

"Some city public school and a bit of strict English-style boarding school gave me my high school diploma and an H.L. Menken-kind of political philosophy. Four years of flower power in Philadelphia at University of Pennsylvania and I came up with a degree in Art History.

By good fortune I made the acquaintance of Sir Alec Cairncross, Master at St. Peter's College in Oxford University. And through a mutual friend at the College, "Bucky" Fuller, I was "sent up" to read English Language and Literature. My tutors were all huge characters: Francis Warner, protégé to the theater of the absurd that Beckett popularized; and Bob Birchfield, the sometimes controversial editor of the Oxford English Dictionary Supplement.

It was here in the charmed countryside and chalk streams that I feasted on everything British. The Test and Itchen were my learning ground, the Lake district through to the Lochs. Adventure took me further east to the Hill Stations of India in pursuit of Himalayan trout. I fished the marvelous streams of Pahalgam in the Vale of Kashmir.

When I returned to North America my attention turned to the Battenkill, the Willowemec, and the Delaware for the finest in classic trout fishing. One year I topped the catch record in Roscoe with an old brown over 5 pounds from the Beaverkill. In the Florida Keys I fished many years for bonefish, tarpon and the elusive permit; first with Bill Curtis, known for his legendary orneriness and later with Bob Branham, Harry Spears, Rick Ruoff, Stu Apte and Frank Catino. The flats of Elliot Key and Stiltsville have given me many bonefish and even a few grand-slams.

Now my son and I take annual trips to the Bahamas where wading the white sands of the Bahamas takes our fancy. My wife

Lynda helps with the recipes and menus for the camp, as well as consults on the design and general welfare. All four of my children have caught salmon on a fly and love camp."

Steve Latner's business interests are in real estate (He says, "I like to ruin neighborhoods with high-rise buildings, but never ruin arable land."), the diagnostic laboratory testing industry (His company, Dynacare is the second largest in Canada), and "many other hair-brain schemes."

Steven Latner and his Sevogle Salmon Club crew, to be certain accomplish a culinary feat, and much more.

There are, in wilderness fishing camps, certain persistent philosophies on cuisine: Basic, fill up the sports with lots of food, screw flavor, it's more important that everyone has mountains to eat: Available, the clients would like to eat fish, but there are too few trout to both eat and fish for, so feed them all pike, continuously. Labor-intensive: if it's difficult to acquire in the bush, the clients will be impressed and feel they're getting their money's worth, so fly it in. These philosophies each have their good points. It is important to make sure the folks aren't hungry, or eat the endangered fish and, yes, it's a kick to have ice cream when there's no refrigeration. Sometimes these philosophies overlap, too, and have for me produced some wonderful meals, such as fresh Pacific salmon sushi.

But Steve, his wife Lynda, Frenchy, the Camp's head guide and manager, and the Camp's chef, Chantal, have gone far beyond the usual philosophy of what to feed the guests.

We visited the Sevogle Salmon Club last Fall, at the end of the salmon runs and at the start of woodcock season in New Brunswick. We were greeted car-side with a glass of single-malt scotch and then inside the lodge with hors d'oeuvre of woodcock and Atlantic salmon. After hot showers, dinner accelerated into lobster tail salad, lentil soup, grilled roast of lamb and tiny vegetables along with grated white truffle, some chocolate and raspberry dessert with a Stilton and fruit platter. All courses were accented, both in the cooking and at the table, with the proper liquors and wines, even a wonderful dessert ice wine from Ontario's Niagara Peninsula. But I was most intoxicated with the execution of it all, from the perfection of its flavor; we were consuming for reasons beyond mere bodily sustenance.

Much of what is accomplished at a Sevogle Club meal comes from attention to detail. Steve writes me that they maintain three different types of outdoor cookers; a silo-style water smoker, a kettle grill, and a Texas-style drum barbecue. All three styles are available in order to mix and match in one meal just the right cooking technique for the creation of multiple flavor sensations. Then there is the science of the woods to use for kindling or smoking; cherry and apple for the slow, smoky long cooking, oak for the traditional Scottish smoked salmon. It is all so carefully thought out.

But in the end what really makes the Sevogle Club so very good is not the detail or even the specific ingredients; it is that very basic understanding that we all, all of us who hunt and fish, have an almost primordial desire to eat from the wild, to fully experience the taste sensations of the land and waters we visit and partake of. At the Sevogle Salmon Club the dinners are not only brimming with New Brunswick gifts from nature, but each item is truly treated with the respect such a precious gift demands — the result is a very complete, fulfilling experience.

And then, to accentuate such perfection, the rarest of foods: Fresh, white truffles from Italy are brought in. I know, I know, these are not natives to New Brunswick's wild foods, but if it were a choice between white truffles from Italy and tubs of ice cream . . . well. It's really just because the aroma of white truffles reminds me of the pungent smell of sweet, damp earth. I promise.

SMOKED SALMON

2 -4 grilse fillets with skin
Brine:
>   1 quart water
>   ¼ cup salt
>   1 teaspoon soy sauce
>   ¼ cup brandy

Soak the fillets skin side down completely covered in brine for several hours. Drain fillets and place them skin side down on the rack at the far end of a drum-style barbecue. Build a charcoal fire in its attached firebox. Add fresh cut green fruit wood and smoke for 3 to 6 hours (depending on thickness and number of fillets) at approximately 160°. A chimney-vent controls the smoke and temperature.

TEMMY'S SALMON CROQUETTES

2 cups fresh cooked salmon
¼-½ cup dried bread crumbs or matzo meal
2 eggs
2-3 shallots or scallions
1 red pepper, chopped finely
1 small cooked potato, chopped
1 tablespoon chopped fresh dill
1 teaspoon honey mustard
1 tablespoon fresh lemon juice
½ teaspoon salt
½ pepper
Butter

Sauté the shallots in a little butter until translucent. Cut the cooked salmon into small pieces. Add eggs, sautéed shallots, dill, lemon juice, honey mustard, salt, pepper, red pepper, potato and bread crumbs and blend until smooth. Form into small croquettes (small burger-size patties). Chill for 30 minutes or longer. Melt butter in a large, heavy skillet and fry over medium heat. Cook about three minutes each side until crispy and serve with Dill Mayonnaise.

DILL MAYONNAISE

1 cup mayonnaise
¼ cup plain yogurt
4 green onions, chopped
1 tablespoon capers
1 tablespoon fresh dill, chopped fine
2 teaspoon Dijon mustard
2 teaspoons prepared white horseradish
1 tablespoon fresh lemon juice

Combine all ingredients well.

LOBSTER

1½-2 pound lobsters (1 per person)
Salt
Place the lobsters in boiling water for 1 ½ minutes, remove and dry. Crack shell. Prepare the grill and when hot, barbecue the lobsters until done.

CHANTAL'S LOBSTER ROE SAUCE

½ cup of mayonnaise
1 tablespoon Dijon mustard
⅓ cup chopped chives
1 teaspoon tarragon
¼ cup lobster roe
1 garlic clove, finely chopped
Splash of white wine
Lemon juice to taste

Mix all the ingredients and refrigerate for at least 1 hour.

SMOKED OYSTERS

2 dozen oysters
½ pound butter
1 garlic clove, finely minced
¼ teaspoon cayenne pepper
2 lemons

Melt the butter and mix with the juice of the two lemons, garlic and cayenne pepper. Let simmer together for a few minutes. Then let the mixture steep for a while.

Shuck the oysters and drizzle about half a teaspoon of the sauce into each shell.

When the grill is ready distribute the oysters on the grill and close the hood. Cook and smoke for 10 to 15 minutes. Serve immediately.

KARL MALONE

Karl Malone was drafted by the Utah Jazz in 1985 out of Louisiana Tech; since then he has missed only four games in his NBA career and never a playoff game. Karl currently holds the NBA playoff record for highest scoring average among active players with an average of 27.3 points a game. He has been named eight times to the All-NBA First Team and has played in nine NBA All-Star games (1988-1996). He was named MVP in the 1989 Houston All-Star game and Co-MVP (with Jazz teammate John Stockton) in 1993 of the Salt Lake City All-Star game. In addition, Karl has been a member of both the 1992 and the 1996 Olympic Basketball Teams representing the U.S. in Barcelona and Atlanta.

In addition to his basketball career, Karl has opened a sports apparel store in Salt Lake. In 1993 he had a special portable sports shop built; this store is housed in a trailer that Karl can haul around in his custom built Freightliner semi-truck, distinguished by the personalized western scene paint job.

Karl and his wife Kay, a former Miss Idaho USA, are both very active in children's charities such as: the NBA's Healthy Families America program; local and national Prevention of Child Abuse programs, D.A.R.E; and Drug Free Red Ribbon Week. They are currently raising funds for a Children's Justice Center and Kay sits on the Board of Directors for Utah's Special Olympics.

The Malones have three children and live not only in Salt Lake but have a ranch in Arkansas where Karl can do much of his hunting and fishing. Karl is an avid outdoorsman; in fact, he considers himself better with a reel, rod and a rifle than with a basketball.

K arl Malone is my idol. Not because it's in vogue to idolize sports heroes, or because he's an outstanding basketball player and basketball has been a longtime, favorite sport with me, or because he's such a decent human being. No, he's the best to me because he's a fishing maniac — and a great basketball player...and a nice guy.

Several years ago, Ed was writing an article for *Esquire Sportsman* and had a long conversation with Karl. Karl was supposed to be relating his most memorable fishing story; but, as can happen with two soul-mates, the conversation revealed much more than just a nice day on the river. Karl talks:

"Well, what I do for a living, as you know, is very stressful and time-consuming and all that. Ever since I was a little kid I always saw and read in the history books about Alaska, and great fishing. I always read that all my life. And I always heard about Canada. I'm from Louisiana. And I always heard about Idaho. Fishing in those three places: I thought that if I ever got there, I would be in heaven. Being from Louisiana, from a town of 200 people, as a little kid I knew of no way possible I could ever be there.

"And what happened? I got drafted by Utah. Now I'm close to Idaho! I never knew I would meet my wife from Idaho, but hey...Then all of a sudden, I take my first trip to Alaska. Then I take my first trip to Canada. And you know what? It was everything and more than I dreamed of.

"I dreamed of putting on my waders and standing in the streams while the sockeye salmon were running. And I dreamed of that in about 2 or 3 feet of water and they're running over your waders, still going upstream.

"I did that. I actually did that. And to me, I thought, I had died and gone to heaven. I felt it was 'it.'

"I've got property in Idaho. My wife is from Idaho Falls. We've got about 23 acres right in Swan Valley, on the river...where we're going to put a little cabin. On 20 (of the acres) that's just raw land that we're going to one day build a fishing lodge for when I retire. I have a ranch back in Arkansas that I've stocked pretty neat with bass.

"See, I guess I'm a dreamer. Like I tell my wife, I could never buy too many fishing rods, too many guns, to hunt with and to fish with because I'm an outdoorsman. And I tell her I could never buy too many pickup trucks.

"You know I dream about when I retire and get my children up while they're half asleep and put them in the truck while they're still asleep and wake 'em when we get where we're going. And I love it.

"What I'm doing with my property in Arkansas, and I guess the most important thing about me, is I guess I'm an environmentalist, so to speak, because the most disheartening thing to me is: Whatever happened to all the great hunting and fishing places? Now you've got poaching and all that stuff.

"With my property in Arkansas now, I'm restocking all my ponds. I'm building a big pond this year to preserve all the habitat. And I'm building another 3 to 4 acre pond and I'm hoping to import 3 or 4,000 Florida bass and put them in there.

"On one of the ponds now we have bream. Nesting. You know what I did? I took my fly rod home and put those popping bugs on. Oh, my God. Threw it right on top of the nest, and sort of twitched it a couple of times. When those bream hit that fly rod — Oh, my God.

"I bought that parcel of property (in Arkansas) and I raise cattle on it. I'd been grooming the owner for 3 or 4 years to buy it, and he didn't give in too easily. He said, 'I'll tell you what. You win the gold medal, and I'll sell you the property.' So we won the gold medal.

"I've had one or two opportunities to do fishing shows, but they never fit in. You know what I do on Sundays? If I sleep in on Sundays, or whatever? I wake up and turn on TNN and watch Bill Dance and all of those guys on the fishing shows. I think I know that Wal-mart commercial by heart.

"You know there are just certain things that are important to me and certain things that I always wish I could do. It's not a dream of mine to fly on the Concorde, to go to London for dinner. You know what I'm saying? Stuff like that. It is a dream of mine to meet people like him (Bill Dance) that I think are...you know...that understand why you're alive. Yeah."

Karl's recipe was actually given to me while Karl was away in Atlanta winning the second gold medal (let's hope he gets another parcel of Arkansas land out of the deal.) It's not exactly a fish recipe, but I thought seafood counted. And besides, it's taken from the Utah Jazz cookbook, the proceeds from which go to charity.

Yeah, I believe Karl Malone truly knows why he's alive.

KARL'S HOT CRAB SALAD

2 fresh heads of lettuce
6 boiled eggs, chopped
2 cucumbers, chopped
2 cups raisins
Chopped green onions
1 stick (8 tablespoons) butter
4 lemons, squeezed
1 large bottle (24-ounces) of ranch dressing
12-ounce bag of shredded cheddar cheese
2 pounds of large crab flakes

In a large mixing bowl, toss together lettuce, eggs, cucumbers, green onions, and raisins and put to the side.

Place a stick of butter in a medium sauce pan and melt. Add squeezed lemon juice and let simmer on low.

In a medium sauce pan, heat the entire bottle of ranch dressing along with the cheddar cheese. Let simmer on low after the cheese has melted.

Heat the crab flakes in a microwave on high for up to 5 minutes.

Mix butter and lemon juice, Ranch dressing and melted cheese together. Add crab flakes to lettuce mixture. Just before serving, top with heated dressing and eat warm.

TERRY MCDONELL

Terry McDonell was named editor-in-chief and publisher of *Sports Afield*, the oldest outdoor magazine in America, in 1993. He is one of the most respected names in outdoor publishing, having been the first editor of *Outside* magazine and the founder of *Rocky Mountain* magazine.

Terry moved to *Sports Afield* after serving three years as editor-in-chief of *Esquire* where he started *Esquire Sportsman*, *Esquire Gentleman* and edited *Lust, Violence, Sin and Magic: Sixty Years of Esquire Fiction*. While under Terry's editorship at *Esquire*, the magazine received numerous accolades and awards from the National Magazine Awards and won the Livingston Award for National Reporting.

Prior to *Esquire*, he was president and editor of *Smart*, a magazine he founded in 1988. Earlier he was managing editor of *Rolling Stone* and assistant managing editor of *Newsweek*.

Also a novelist and screenwriter, Terry's television writing credits include "Miami Vice" and "China Beach." His novel, *California Bloodstock*, was published in 1980 by Macmillan and then reissued by Vintage Contemporaries in 1989.

In addition, Terry wrote the best-selling video game "Night Trap" which was converted to CD-Rom in 1992. In 1994 he was host of MCA's nightly, nationally-syndicated talk show "Last Call."

T erry McDonell used to be disconcerting to me, for a lot of reasons. I'd gotten off to an unfortunate start with him when he was editor of *Esquire* by trying to sell him an article and misspelling his name in my query letter. He also has that unnerving mannerism common to editors which is to respond to your questions with long silent pauses or short, curt, one-word answers — like "no." And then, of course, there's his formidable career and the fact that he really is one of the best editors around. I could never figure out exactly what it was about Terry that made him such a great editor until I went fishing with him.

We were visiting our friends, Charles and Patricia Gaines, in Nova

Scotia and Terry had come for a visit, too, with his two young sons, Nick and Thomas. The boys were what I imagined male versions of Eloise to be; smart, precocious city kids who had the energy and athleticism of 100 race horses. They were wonderful, although exhausting, and the game for the adults came to be how to focus all this energy. Charles took them to the gym to work out with him, Terry bought fireworks to set off, and then there was a bass fishing trip, an overnight to a remote set of lakes. A friend of Charles,' Perry Munro, ran a hunting and fishing lodge and would provide guides, boats, motors, cabin, any necessary rods, and a planked salmon for dinner. It was a fair drive, but we got to the lakes in time to have a few hours of evening to fish. Terry went with Nick and Thomas and Perry's son as guide in one boat. Ed, Charles, Perry and I went in a second boat. The boys would spin fish, and perhaps try their hand at a fly rod, so the sense was to let them have their space. We lost track of them for a while; and as that perfect fishing time at dusk turned to black night and we had had our successes with the smallmouth, we headed back to shore catching a glimpse of the McDonell boat. I thought one of the boys looked wet and when we came up close to them there was some long explanation and series of apologies about the loss of, what turned out to be Perry's favorite and rather expensive spinning gear. It had gone overboard with the kid and it had seemed more important to Terry to save his son; although I wasn't certain that was the universally felt priority of the group. The tension was a bit heavy for a while. But Terry gracefully struck the balance between good father and good guest by not saying much but reimbursing and apologizing to Perry; yet not overdoing it to the point of making Nick feel worse than he already did.

I realized that Terry was a very nice dad. And it's probably some of those intuitive nice dad qualities that also makes him a great editor. Patience, of course, but also a sense of loyalty to the smaller guy. He is the writer's advocate (and, naturally his children's, too), yet never forsakes honesty. And he knows exactly the essential point: Let the kid make his mistakes and let a writer's work maintain its integrity. Oh, and yes, he knows the essential point to grilling fish, too: Always plan the recipe to incorporate cocktail time into it.

WHEN FISHERMEN COOK FISH

TERRY MCDONELL'S SWORDFISH

2-4 swordfish steaks cut thick, 1" to 2"
¼ cup Worcestershire sauce
½ cup green olive oil
2 cloves garlic, chopped fine
1 tablespoon lemon juice
1 tablespoon chopped chives
Tabasco
Salt (garlic salt if you like a lot of garlic) and pepper

In a bowl combine the Worcestershire sauce, olive oil, chopped garlic, lemon juice, chives and Tabasco sauce to taste (remembering that Tabasco intensity increases over time) and make any adjustments. Place the swordfish steaks (one per person) in a small shallow baking dish and pour the marinade over them. Let sit for approximately one hour while you have a cocktail and get the charcoal hot. Turn the steaks at least once. Paint the grill with some of the marinade and lay the steaks on. Salt and pepper the steaks on both sides as they cook. Cook rare.

PATRICK F. MCMANUS

Pat McManus is a writer whose genius is his humor. Pat has said of humor writers, "As soon as the humor writer starts thinking of himself as a person of letters, as soon as he perceives his purpose as something other than seeking the ultimate, base, vulgar, gut-busting, psyche-wrenching laugh, he is done for. I have been chided by some reviewers for not possessing a more serious comic purpose. To provoke the uniquely human phenomenon of laughter is, it seems to me, a serious comic purpose, provided, of course, there is such a thing as a serious comic purpose."

He was born and raised in Idaho, and received his BA from Washington State University. After college he became a newspaper reporter for the *Daily Olympian* and then in 1960 for KREM-TV . For 23 years he taught English and Journalism at Eastern Washington University.

His magazine articles have appeared in *Reader's Digest*, *TV Guide*, *Sports Illustrated*, *Field & Stream*, *Outdoor Life*, *New York Times* and many others.

Pat has written many books including *How I Got This Way*; *The Good Samaritan Strikes Again*; *Real Ponies Don't Oink*; *The Night the Bear Ate Goombaw*; *Whatchagot Stew: a memoir of an Idaho childhood, with recipes and commentaries*; *Rubber Legs and White Tail-hairs*; *The Grasshopper Trap*; *Never Sniff a Gift Fish*; *A Fine and Pleasant Misery*; a kids humor book entitled *Kid Camping from AAAAIIII to Zip*; and *They Shoot Canoes, Don't They?* He most recently authored *Never Cry "Arp."* In addition he has been an associate editor of *Field & Stream* and is currently editor-at-large of *Outdoor Life*.

P at McManus professes not to be a cook; he also says that the purpose of his humor is solely to make people laugh. Well, who's to argue — especially after reading his "recipe." But then again, I think there's a bit more here than mere proof of his ineptitude around the cook fire and a few giggles. Like all great humorists the big laughs come from revealing certain ultimate truths; and what could be more of an ultimate truth than the fact that the best cooked trout involves no other ingredients than a fresh trout and a little grease. There is no need for a real recipe. Actually, I guess there's no need for a cookbook.

I did consider editing Pat's recipe out of the book since he can't cook and his little recipe is really not all that funny. Just remember that he doesn't take himself too seriously. So don't you either.

TROUT FLAMBÉ

2 trout per person
3-4 strips of bacon
1 mountain trout stream
1 sandy or rocky beach
1 large square of aluminum foil
1 creel
1 jack knife
1 flashlight

Catch and clean trout. After dark, build driftwood fire on beach. Fire should not be so large as to singe eyebrows beyond radius of four feet.

Shape aluminum foil into frying pan.

Remove bacon from creel. Wipe off marinade of trout juices. Lay in frying pan. Heat until grease sizzles.

Place trout in pan with bacon. Place trout in pan with bacon. Arrange rocks so pan doesn't collapse and dump trout in fire again. Wipe trout on pants to remove sand, ashes, grease, and residue of eyebrows and arm hair. Place back in pan. Soak fingers in stream until firm and cool.

Shine flashlight directly down into pan while turning trout with jack knife. Proximity of fingers to hot grease will instantly ignite grease, thus achieving the desired flambé effect.

Smother flames with handy article of clothing. Turn trout. Don't be concerned if skin flakes off body. This is normal. It will grow back in a month or so, with only minor scar tissue.

Trout are done when either they or you are brown on both sides. Serve.

PETER MITCHELL MILLER

Peter Miller's biography lists his occupation since 1964 as free-lance photographer-writer. Before that he was a reporter-writer for *LIFE* magazine; he started his career as a photographer's assistant to Yousuf Karsh. Peter's work has appeared in *Sports Illustrated, Smithsonian, New York Times Sunday Magazine, Ski, Snow Country, Field & Stream, Travel & Leisure, Gray's Sporting Journal*, most in-flight magazines and many foreign publications.

Peter has authored five books; *The 30,000 Mile Ski Race, The Skier's Almanac, The Photographer's Almanac, Vermont People*, and *People of the Great Plains*. He has received several awards including the Lifetime Achievement in Journalism from the International Association of Ski History and Award for Visual Excellence from the Image Bank.

Peter's biography explains that he was born in 1934 at 1:45 a.m., a Capricorn with a Scorpio rising, in a New York hospital born to a Wall Street Banker and an Irish feminist. Presently an orphan. He graduated from high school at Burr and Burton Seminary in Vermont where he had skipped school for two weeks to go deer hunting and then had his rifles stolen. He used the insurance money to buy cameras.

Peter says he was a lazy student and cruised through the University of Toronto only on what the Benedictine monks had taught him in high school; he took pictures to help pay his way through college. In his junior year Peter worked as an assistant to Yousuf Karsh as Karsh photographed the famous people in Europe. "Caught Lord Mountbatten in his skivvies, almost poisoned with rotten food by Albert Schweitzer, Picasso smoked all my cigarettes, Dame Edith Evans got me drunk." After two years in the Army as a GI photographer in Paris, France, Peter one again worked for Karsh and "decided I never again would be anyone's assistant. Refused to kiss Pope John's ring and gave up religion based on the history of the Catholic Church in the suppression and manipulation of the masses (actually, I'm a pagan at heart)."

Peter then fulfilled his high school ambition of working for *LIFE* magazine as a writer-photographer. "Scooped the nation on the sinking of the Thresher submarine. Scoop got suppressed by *LIFE*. Quit and moved to Vermont." He started his own ski magazine ("lost my shirt on that venture"), then wrote and photographed for magazines and was an editor at *SKI* until he quit ("sick of bureaucratic editors...was hated by *SKI* magazine staff") and began doing stock photography seriously. "Happiest when skiing in the high Alps, fly fishing in Montana, or going some place I haven't been before."

In 1993 Peter started work on his latest book, *People of the Great Plains*. He spent seven months towing a 17', 1968 Airstream camper 35,000 miles through the high plains west of the 98th Meridian. "Rancher in North Dakota said I was like the Dodo bird that flies backwards — knows where it's been, but not where it's going." *People of the Plains* was turned down by 22 publishers, but then in 1995 Peter was granted a $25,000 award to finish the book, which he did.

Peter Miller is, to a woman, the kind of photographer she might beg to photograph her in the nude, profess undying love to and, if she has a brain in her head, would refuse all marriage proposals or offers of a long term relationship. No, he is very definitely not the real life character from whom the Bridges' Kincaid was cloned, Peter's far too irreverent. He simply happens to be a photographer capable of making a naked Rosanne Barr appear beautiful, possesses a kind of macho independence edged ever so slightly in vulnerability and, first and foremost, inspires indiscretion. Unfortunately, he verges on being hyperactive and, while accomplishing a bunch of really cool stuff, he's never around. Plus he's far too bachelored and damaged from former lovers/wives to now bother figuring how to incorporate a woman into the cool stuff.

Peter always talks straight-forwardly and certainly reveals plenty of himself in his writings here; except for refusing to state plainly those extreme levels of sensitivity he most certainly carries within. In general, he does a pretty good job concealing his sensibilities until you look at one of his photographs, read his books, fish with him or until he talks about food. At least for me, he's exposed through the food conversation. He knows the perfect wine, the right herbs and better yet he knows before anyone else the best places in the world to catch the tastiest trout or most delectable woodcock. As I said, he inspires indiscretion.

"In the early 1980s, before Californians discovered Montana and before the 'River Runs Through It' ruined trout fishing, I and a couple of friends made our annual trip to Ennis, Montana in the Stone Fly; a decrepit motorized box called an RV that liked to lose its brakes on very steep passes. It took us 51 hours to drive from Stowe, Vermont to Ennis, where we camped in a state-run campsite called the Valley Garden. We were known locally as the woodchucks who made our reputation in the bars with our inability to handle numerous shots of cheap tequila chased with a can of Coors. Our group included Ted Ross, owner of Stone Fly, who displayed an uncanny ability with dispatching a jug of vodka; Peter Ruscph, who was so paranoid about not having fish attached to his rod we called him Chief Crazy Rod; Tony Thompson, WASP; and Matt Forelli from Connecticut. Matt assumed his position as Capo and once warned me, when I rented an apartment in New York from him that, if I didn't pay the rent, his cousin Charley, who sucked lollipops and carried a .357 magnum, would pay me a visit to measure my feet.

"Our favorite fishing was in the channels below the Valley Gardens. Hardly any one fished there for it was a couple of miles to walk down and we had to cross the Madison, which could be very tricky in late June if the snowpack had been deep. Sometimes we would cross arm-in-arm to avoid being shoved by the current into doing 'The Madison Mambo.' It wasn't unusual for us to fish down to the Brown and Rainbow pools (known only to us), where sometimes we would catch a dozen fish over 18" in a feverish half-hour at late dusk.

"We'd come back in the dark, fighting the currents and hoping we were in the right channel. We had a couple of spots we considered safe to cross the Madison and, believe me, doing that successfully in pitch dark is one of the major accomplishments of my life.

"This era was before the politically correct anglers ruined our sport and we could keep a fish or two for dinner. We experienced the Madison River, with its fervid insect life and cold waters, and which produced browns and rainbows with a textured orange flesh of a delicacy most gourmets would now never experience.

"Dinner was often at 11:00 p.m. over a campfire ringed with river stones and covered with an iron grate. We would clean the fish, stuff the cavity with dollops of butter and wedges of lemon, salt and pepper inside and outside, wrap it in tin foil (actually aluminum foil, but the term indicates our age) and lay it on the grate. With it we would have tin foil baked potatoes cooked in the fire and corn-on-the-cob cooked still in the husks with the husks wetted down.

"The tin foil poaches the trout. The time to cook the trout was long enough to get a little buzz on, then we would open the tin foil, fillet the trout and portion it out. Actually the trout was an hors d'oeuvre; we often followed up with whatever Chief Crazy Rod was into that night — usually grilled chicken.

"I don't recall where this Arctic char recipe came from. It was written down by me a long time ago and I found it stuck in my LaRousse Gastronomique. I know the recipe comes from the late 1970s, when I returned from a photo assignment at Pangnirtung in the Northwest Territories. From Pangnirtung we boarded a commercial fishing boat and we weaved our way north of the Arctic Circle into the midnight sun. We were weaving because there were so many icebergs to avoid that one of the Inuit mates climbed the mast and gave hand signals to chart our course. Half the town came along and we watched an Inuit shoot a duck on the fly with a .30-06 (pure damned luck, judging from the smile on his face) and a canoe chase for the Beluga white whale. The real purpose, though, was to fish for Arctic char, which were abundant and too easy to catch in a cove that was used thousands of years ago by the Barrow culture."

ARCTIC CHAR WITH SAUCE VERTE

1 Arctic char
2 cups water
2 cups white wine
2 bay leaves
2 bunches of watercress
24 spinach leaves
1 pint sour cream
Juice from a lemon
Juice from a lime
Dash of Tabasco
1 teaspoon Worcestershire sauce
Pinch of nutmeg
Pinch of garlic salt

Pouch the char in the water, wine and bay leaves for about 10 minutes while you make the sauce. Dump the watercress, spinach, sour cream, juice from the lemon and lime, Tabasco, Worcestershire sauce, nutmeg, and garlic salt in a blender. Blend the hell out of it, leave it in the blender, put in the refrigerator and chill. You can warm this sauce to cover a freshly poached char or salmon; but I like it best chilled and blanketing a cold salmon or char. It is best not to serve an ordinary wine with this delicacy. I prefer a Meursault or, if you can find it and you are watching your pennies, a Beaujolais Blanc, which has a flinty character. When I'm in the chips, I've taken to sharing this dish with a bottle of Pol Roger.

BLUEFISH VIA SOUTHWEST OF
AMERICA AND MEXICO TO LONDON

1 snapper bluefish (small size) fillet
1 pint sour cream or crème fraîche
2-3 chipotles with juice (chipotles are jalapeños peppers smoked
    and packed in their own juices)
2-3 tablespoons chives or parsley

Blend the sour cream, chipotles and chives and spread on the bluefish fillet. Grill for 10 minutes; 5 with the lid on and 5 with it off. Last time we had this dish it was accompanied with fresh string beans blanched in boiling water and tossed lightly with a little sesame oil; and slices of beef tomatoes and red onions sprinkled with capers and drizzled with a nice vinaigrette made from Dijon mustard, a clove of crushed garlic, balsamic vinegar and olive oil.

TOM MONTGOMERY

After Tom Montgomery finished his formal education at Middlebury College and Oxford University he began to split his time between guiding and photography. His professional travels have taken him to such remote areas as New Zealand, Argentina, Chile, and Nepal. He also guides and photographs closer to his home of Jackson Hole, Wyoming, with much of his work experience spent in the Rocky Mountain states and Alaska. *The Nature of Flyfishing* is Tom's first book. His photographs have also appeared in many national publications such as *Forbes FYI, Sports Afield, Men's Journal, Esquire Sportsman* and *Gray's Sporting Journal.*

Tom Montgomery and I have been on several photo shoots together, but I have never fished with him as a friend or as a client. I believe he would be an outstanding fishing companion and guide as he provides such excellent company and smokes good cigars. As a photographer he had the opportunity to be unsettling. Not only because he is photographing you and all your fly line for national publication, but because his solo life style, his profession and his exceptional handsomeness smack ever so slightly of someone nice to entice. Yet his non-intrusive, determined and careful manner has always allowed for acting naturally and to producing beautiful images.

I had a sense of Tom as a fishing guide when we were doing an article together in the Bahamas. Our first morning out Tom was busy photographing the Bahamian guide, the setting and me. And the guide was busy trying to help me cast to bonefish in weather that was to become labeled "the storm of the century." This young guide thought the way to show me how to cast in the gale-force winds was to take my rod and cast continually himself until he hooked or harassed the fish. Then he'd hand the rod back to me either to play the fish or try to hook it myself. He would do this while explaining that bonefish were a "mellowtating" kind of fish that were made nervous by stormy weather and flies . . . unless the fly was placed 4" in front of its mouth, mon. Well, this "mon's" casting into the wind was not helped by the pretty obvious advice or the fact that the guide was doing all the fishing.

The weather did not improve, in fact it worsened and stayed nearly unfishable and unphotographable for two weeks. I was out one relatively calm morning with Tom trying to get something on film for the story; winds were only at about 20 mph. We chatted and waded until the moment came when a bonefish appeared and I was to cast to it. Tom's shutter clicked away. I couldn't reach the fish, the wind crumpled the fly line at every cast and I began muttering to the stupid "mellowtating" fish. "Come over here," Tom said. I thought his request was for photographic purposes, but by moving a half circle I got closer to the fish and the wind direction then helped lay the fly line out correctly. I did not catch that bonefish; but soon after I did. I had learned to position myself according to my casting ability, albeit limited. A ridiculously simply piece of advice, really. Something a born fisherman does naturally. But to this overly-instructed and somewhat rigid fly fisherman moving in order to get a bet-ter casting angle hadn't occurred. Moving might frighten the fish away! (Stupid I know, since not moving virtually guaranteed the fish would get away.) Tom's advice was critical and he dished it out with great aplomb, never making me feel silly. He taught me the value of improvisation when fishing.

But of course, improvisation is important when cooking, too. It seemed so appropriate that when I asked Tom where he had learned the following recipe he said, "Oh, I invented it."

GLENLIVET TROUT

1 lake trout gutted but with head left on
¼ pound (1 stick) unsalted butter
2 tablespoon dill
Salt and pepper
1 cup single-malt scotch (the pettier the better)

Season the lake trout cavity and several pats of butter, salt, pepper and the dill. In a large skillet with a lid, pan fry the lake trout in the remaining butter for several minutes turning it once. Pour on the single-malt scotch and cover, letting the fish poach in the liquor until done (about 20 minutes).

DAN AND KRIS O'BRIEN

Kris and Dan O'Brien live in the Black Hills of South Dakota. Kris is an anesthesiologist at Rapid City Regional Hospital and Dan writes novels and non-fiction on a cattle ranch in the Northern Hills.

Dan won the Iowa Short Story Fiction Award in 1986 for his first book, *Eminent Domain*. Since then he has published four books; *The Rites of Autumn: A Falconer's Journey Across the American West*, *Spirit of the Hills*, *The Center of the Nation* and his most recent novel, *Brendan Prairie* from Scribners, 1996. Dan has taught at the University of Colorado and Bowling Green State University and received two fellowships from the National Endowment for the Arts. He also has been awarded an honorary Ph.D. from the University of South Dakota.

When the writing comes slow Dan tends to his ranch chores, flies falcons, fly fishes, or rides horses . . . or all four. Both Kris and Dan fly fish in fresh and saltwater every chance they get. Kris usually does the cooking; Dan eats pretty well.

Kris and Dan O'Brien are the first couple we've ever met who do what we do: Fly fish; hunt; read; have pointing dogs; write for a living; work in hospitals; like to travel; drink martinis and red wine; attend graduate schools at Dartmouth; grew up in the Midwest; hold dear the New Brunswick woodcock hunt; use Tom Montgomery as a photographer — and there's more. In particular it's nice to know another wife who both fly fishes and hunts and is very able at both. I've never minded being the only woman in camp; but women in camp are the male rationale for infusing civility into the living conditions. And it's good to have another woman share the burden of that responsibility with such a semblance in attitude to my own. It's also nice to know another husband besides Ed who's happy to have his wife hunting and fishing with him. Dan and Ed really go on very few hunting and fishing trips without us, and that's their choice. They are truly the most liberated of husbands.

Yes, there are some differences between us all: Dan and Kris don't

scuba dive, and never want to; we don't run cattle, and never want to —
there are only three divorces among the four of us. But the mixture of
like and not-alike has provided a great start on a long-term friendship. I
say start because we've only known them a few years . . . and we've never
been fishing with them.

Fishing is, of course, a critical element to a friendship and quite
frankly I was a tiny bit apprehensive about whether there might be such
a difference in our fishing philosophies as to deaden the fire of this new
friendship. I got a hint of that possibility when I asked them for fish
recipes for this book. "No, we don't really cook fish. We don't have any
recipes." What does that mean, don't cook fish? I know catch-and-release
is very important and very much practiced out West where they live, but
there are saltwater fish, too. And killing a fish every now and then, and
more if it's plentiful, to eat is, after all, at the heart of why we all began
to fish in the first place.

This could have been a major problem until I realized that "we" really meant I — Dan was talking. Dan doesn't have any recipes because Dan
doesn't cook. Well, Ed doesn't really have recipes either. Maybe they're
not quite as liberated as I thought.

No matter, I like to cook and clearly so does Kris.

O'BRIEN CONCH CEVICHE

8 ounces of conch, scallops or a firm white fish such as halibut
⅓ cup fresh lime juice
2 tomatoes, peeled and diced
½ cup plain or spicy tomato juice
¼ cup chopped red onion
¼ cup sliced green olives
3 tablespoon olive oil
¼ cup orange juice
1 teaspoon chopped jalepeño pepper
½ bay leaf
3 tablespoons cilantro
Salt and pepper

Cut the conch (let someone else get it out of the shell and "tender-
ize" it) into ¼" cubes and marinate in lime juice for 1 hour. This, in
effect, cooks it. Pour off the lime juice, combine all remaining ingredi-

ents, and toss together. Refrigerate for a minimum of 1 hour, but no more than 6 before serving. Garnish with more cilantro and serve alone, or with crackers or chips.

SALMON MOUSSE

2 cups finely chopped poached or smoked salmon
1 envelope unflavored gelatin
¼ cup cold water
½ cup boiling water
½ cup mayonnaise
1 tablespoon lemon juice
1 tablespoon minced shallots
1 teaspoon salt
2 tablespoons chopped fresh dill
¾ cup heavy cream
Tabasco

Soften the gelatin in cold water. Stir in boiling water and let cool. Whisk in the mayonnaise, lemon juice, shallot, salt, dill and a dash of Tabasco. Stir and then let chill in the refrigerator until slightly thickened, about twenty minutes; whip the heavy cream while you wait. Now fold in the salmon into the gelatin mixture and then separately fold in the whipped cream. Pour into a 6 to 8 cup bowl and refrigerate for 4 hours. Serve with toast rounds.

DAVE PERKINS

Dave Perkins is senior vice-president of the Orvis Company, and
has had opportunities to hunt and fish throughout the world. He
learned this recipe while guiding in southeast Idaho during his
college days. To date, he confesses, it is still his favorite recipe;
when cooking at home (Manchester, Vermont) he will often start
a fire in the front yard to make sure he doesn't screw it up.

He writes, "It's about all I have for fish recipes. I'm not big on
cooking fish and the fact is I release most of them."

D
ave Perkins was known to us for a long time in name only. And
then it was only as one of the sons of Leigh and Rommie
Perkins, the owners of Orvis. *Gray's Sporting Journal* had been
out of our lives for four years and we'd lost track of what was happening
to some of our former advertisers; we weren't even really aware that Dave
had gone into the business. That was until we ran into Dave and his wife
Gwen at a resort on the island of Guanaja off the coast of Honduras.

The resort where we were all staying, Posada del Sol, is an Orvis-
endorsed destination for bonefishing and permit fishing; but really it's
most famous for its scuba diving program. We dove every day, three times
a day and happened to be on the same morning dive boat as Gwen
Perkins, who was training and testing for advance certification in scuba
diving. But where was Dave? Well, maybe he was resting up from the long
trip down here. Or maybe he was fishing, what else would he be doing?

Ed and I had been to Posada del Sol before on assignment for *Men's
Journal* and so enjoyed it we'd returned this trip and brought our teenage
children. When we weren't diving, we'd go out bonefishing; but the fishing was hard that week because of heavy winds and we'd roamed the
island and reef clusters a bit more than usual looking for leeward sides of
the flats where the wind was calmer. I kind of expected to see Dave.
Maybe he'd been fishing so much for business he was sick of it?

Our week was drawing to a close; the Perkins had come a few days after
us and still had a couple days left. We'd not had much of an opportunity to
really get to know Dave; we thought this might be unfortunate . . . Gwen

was sure nice. The day before our departure we happened to have lunch at the same table. Well, it turned out that Dave had been getting his open water certification, initially requiring a fair amount of pool work, but now he could do the three dives a day with Gwen. And he'd been out fishing quite a bit (in places that had been too windy for us). He'd actually caught plenty of bonefish, but was still pursuing the elusive permit. Ed and Dave talked flies. Ed had caught his permit on a crab imitation, Dave had tried one. Ed had caught his early in the morning, in fact it was on our first visit to Posada del Sol when we had gotten up each morning at 5:00 a.m. to fish and then returned by 9:00 to meet the diveboat for a three-dive day. But this schedule was a working schedule — we were there for work — it was not vacation-like or meant for wimps, you had to really want to do this. I could see Dave taking this all in and thinking.

The next morning we left very early on the boat to get over to the part of the island where the airstrip was. Twenty minutes into the trip Ed tapped me on the shoulder and pointed across the water to a figure standing on the flat not far from where Ed had caught his permit. The sun was just barely coming up and it was hard to really see who it was until we saw this long lovely cast; we knew it was someone who knew what he was doing. Ed turned to me and smiled, "Dave." And I'm hoping, and I'm pretty sure that, it won't be the last time we run into Dave "working."

PERKINS' STREAMSIDE TROUT

2 trout, cleaned and head removed
2 strips of bacon, or squeeze bottle of margarine
1 lemon
½ an onion chopped fine
½ tomato, chopped
Lemon pepper
Foil

Lay out a piece of foil large enough to seal in two trout. Place each trout on the foil and sprinkle all sides heavily with lemon pepper. Lay a strip of bacon along the side of each fish and squeeze the lemon juice over the trout. Leave the remainder of the lemon with the fish. Add the chopped onion and tomato and fold over foil, rolling up all edges to make air tight. Take sealed package and place directly on top of the coals of the fire. I generally judge the cooking time by how much sizzling you hear inside the package. My guess is approximately 10 minutes should do, but it's easy to check by opening the package to see if the trout flakes easily away from the bones.

Instead of bacon, you can use any greasing agent which will allow enough moisture to prevent trout from sticking to the foil and a little bit of steam for cooking. Squeeze bottles of margarine are easy to pack for along the stream and provide an excellent base for poached trout.

STEVE RAJEFF

Steve Rajeff has been the International All-Round Casting Champion 12 times and National All-Round Casting Champion 22 times. Some of the more notable national fly casting records he holds are: double-handed fly distance of 288,' and 190' for the anglers fly distance. In addition, Steve has worked as a fishing guide for four seasons in Bristol Bay, Alaska, and two seasons on the Big Hole River in Montana. He has also been an instructor at the Bahamas Bonefish School on Great Exuma and at the Florida Keys Outfitter-Saltwater Fly Fishing School. Steve is on the Board of Governors for the FFF (Federation of Fly Fishers) Fly Casting Certification.

He has also worked with several of the large fly rod manufacturers in marketing and product design; he is currently with G. Loomis in Woodland, Washington.

S teve Rajeff, as is clearly evidenced by his biography, is an amazing fly caster. But this does not always make for an amazing fisherman; any more than being a great fish cook makes for being a great fisherman. Each of these skills are useful at a different point in the process of being a fisherman; they nicely sandwich the actual catching of a fish, and each enhances the enjoyment of the sport.

Although superior casting technique does not guarantee a good fisherman; it seems to have coupled well in Steve. This is perhaps because the casting is so natural and effortless for Steve, his focus can remain intent on catching the fish. I watched Steve one time when we were fishing in Alaska together. It was a gravel bar lunch scene and Steve was just fooling around. I asked him to give me a few casting lessons, try my rod and see if it was properly balanced, line-weight to rod-weight. I had anticipated being impressed with the distance he could throw the line, but I was not prepared for the small amount of upper body movement he required to make the line go that far. It was the total opposite of my flailing; his controlled, tight, perfectly-timed movements whipped that line straight across the river and caught a Dolly Varden. He smiled for having caught the fish, not for how long he'd cast the line. Just as I smile when I catch a nice fish and know the delectability of dinner is guaranteed.

I suppose Steve and I would both have to confess to being partakers of open-face sandwiches in this fishing meal. I can catch and cook, but struggle at great casting. And Steve, well let's just say he really can cast and he really is a great fisherman . . . and we both grin a lot.

RAJEFF'S SHORELINE SALMON
(Does not work at home)

1 shoreline
50 pounds of driftwood
1 cup Alaskan Boy Scout fluid (gasoline)
1 sockeye salmon fillet (char, silver or chum salmon can be used)
⅓ cube (pound) of butter (bear grease if in season)
1 onion, sliced
½ pound of mushrooms
Salt and pepper

Make fire to suit coals required for cooking — a few weeks of trial and error will do. Lay fillet on aluminum foil, sprinkle with salt and pepper and throw on the butter, onion and mushrooms. Wrap in two layers of foil (do not use more layers, takes too long to cook). With fire burned down to mostly coals, shove fire over with insulated wader boot. Place the foil-wrapped salmon under coals, and re-deposit coals over salmon. Wait 10 minutes. Flip foil-wrapped salmon over. Wait 10 minutes. Call fisherman from stream, ready to serve.

CHET AND PENNY RENESON

Chet Reneson has been a full-time, fine artist for almost 30 years. He has been the Trout Unlimited Artist of the Year, Ducks Unlimited Artist of the Year and the Atlantic Salmon Federation Artist of the Year. In addition, his artwork has appeared in leading magazines such as *Gray's Sporting Journal, Sports Afield* and *Sporting Classics;* his watercolors have also been covers to the L.L. Bean and Frontiers catalogs.

Chet's paintings have been on the front cover of *Gray's Sporting Journal* more than any other artist; 19 times from 1976 to 1991.

Chet and Penny Reneson have been our friends for over 20 years now and it's taken me that long to learn that when it comes to the cooking of wild foods, don't pay any attention to Chet. In one of my earlier cookbooks I related a story about Chet and fiddleheads (those spring-time ferns that have not unfolded and resemble little wheels on the end of a stalk). I wrote:

"Set on always trying to obtain wild food and wanting my children to understand the bounty of the woods, the Gray family set out on an excursion to gather fiddleheads and came home quite successfully with a large basket full. I tried everything I could think of to get the chaff off — from soaking to picking, and finally in desperation, I called my friends the Renesons, who I knew to be fanciers of the vegetable. Unfortunately, Chet answered the phone. When I queried him about how to get the moldy stuff off the fiddleheads he suggested as follows: In the bow of your Grand Laker canoe place your spouse and the basket of fiddleheads. In the stern, seated at the throttle of the 50-horse Johnson, place yourself dressed in black sou'wester and hat. Once untied from the dock, speed boat at full throttle the length of the 10-mile lake with spouse holding up each individual fiddlehead and you dodging the chaff which, hopefully, is flying back at you."

You'd have thought, wouldn't you, I'd learn. Chet telephoned about six months ago and for some unknown reason (I must have been possessed) I mentioned this cookbook and my desire to get recipes from them for fish and then later on for a game cookbook. Chet's a little deaf now and I don't think he heard a word about the fish, "We have this great duck recipe, Penny doesn't like it because it has so much cholesterol in it. But I like it. First you soak the duck in fat. It will take you about a year to collect enough of this fat, fat from all the ducks and geese that are shot on the coast of Connecticut . . ." It was a good thing I was looking for fish recipes.

Penny is innately a good cook. Some of this ability surely comes from her love of wild food, but I think also because she approaches it with the same artistic talent that Chet holds for painting, in 20 years I have learned much from Penny on wild game and fish cooking. Of course, she espouses the simple fish recipe (all of us who fish and cook must) and she has had to learn to remain flexible, as she discusses here in her description of what cooking on a Bahamian island requires.

Actually, when it comes right down to it I think it's years of living with Chet and all that fat and fiddlehead chaff that's provided the best training for flexibility . . . with food, of course. Penny writes me:

"For a person who loves to cook and eat as much as I do, I couldn't have married a man with a better career. Chet Reneson makes his living painting pictures of himself hunting and fishing for all the tasty morsels out there in the wildlife kingdom. And I get to cook and eat it!

"We met in art school where I decided he was a star and needed someone like me to help him develop his career. We've been hunting, fishing and selling paintings and lithographs ever since, for 36 years. We've done a lot of wonderful things all those years, but the best was buying our Grady White for fishing in the Bahamas. Our first trip down was in 1969 and we have missed very few years in between. Recently we have been making the trip two or three times a year. We still love turkey and deer hunting, upland birds with our setter, Atlantic salmon on the North Shore; and all are reproduced in the studio. But the boat is the best.

"On the small island we fish from, fresh produce and the other high-tech cooking ingredients and supplies we have all come to take for granted, are not to be found.

"This makes the cooking challenges more fun and is a fine excuse if your meal doesn't produce the desired effect. It also makes for very simple quick, meals which is the best part at the end of a hot, tiring day in the boat."

DOLPHIN CHOWDER

1 dolphin, cleaned, filleted, with head and tail removed and backbone reserved
1½ quarts water
2 medium-size onions, diced
½ red pepper, diced
½ green pepper
1 large potato, peeled and diced
2 stalks celery, diced
3-4 garlic cloves, diced
4 tablespoons olive oil
1 tablespoon thyme
Squirt of anchovies paste
Salt and pepper

Fillet the meat of both sides of the fish, and skin fillets. Discard the tail, head and skin and place the backbone in a kettle with the water and bring to a boil. Let simmer for 20 minutes. Scrape the meat off the backbone into the liquid, reserve the broth but discard the bones. In a skillet add 2 tablespoons or so of olive oil and sauté the red and green pepper, onion, celery, potato, and garlic for a very few minutes until they are cooked but still crisp. Add the sautéed vegetables to the kettle of fish stock along with the thyme, anchovies paste, and salt and pepper to taste. Cut the dolphin fillets into 2" square chunks and sauté in a hot skillet with the remaining olive oil. Cook it so the outside is seared brown, but the inside remains slightly under-done in center. Gently place the fish in the kettle and return to a very slow simmer. Deglaze pan with a little of the liquid from the kettle and scrape all the good tidbits back into chowder. The whole idea is to keep everything just barely done. Do not boil or over cook. Check for seasoning and sample the potatoes and fish for doneness. Serve.

TROPICAL BRANDY FILLETS

1 wahoo fillet (or grouper, dolphin, or king mackerel), skinned
4-5 tablespoons olive oil
Hot sauce
2 tablespoons crushed garlic cloves
5 tablespoons lime juice
5 tablespoons brandy

Sauté the fillet, or chunks up to 10" long, in olive oil with a couple of splashes of hot sauce. Brown the fish on both sides and remove before completely cooked. Place the fillet in a swallow baking pan or cookie sheet in a 350° oven for about 5 minutes. While the fish is in the oven, add to the sauté pan, the garlic, lime juice and brandy. If there isn't very much oil remaining from cooking the fish, add some, and cook very hot, scraping the pan with a whisk while stirring the liquid. When the fillets are just done (do not over cook – they should be moist and flaky) remove from the oven and onto a platter. Pour/scrape the brandy sauce over the fish and serve.

GRILLED GROUPER

1 grouper fillet (or mackerel, wahoo or jack)
¾ cup olive oil
Juice of 1 lime
3-4 garlic cloves, pressed

Combine the olive oil, lime juice, and garlic and marinate the fillet for ½ an hour or until the coals burn down. Cook the fish over low coals covered with palm frowns that have been rinsed in saltwater and are still wet. Or broil low with a loose piece of foil to cover to keep in the moisture. When the fish is done, remove to a warmed platter. While the fish cooks, here are two ideas for sauces that can be made:

GROUPER SAUCE I

½ of the marinade that you've reserved
½ cup chardonnay
1 tablespoon anchovy paste
2 teaspoons capers

Combine all ingredients and pour over grilled fish.

GROUPER SAUCE II

2 medium-size tomatoes, chopped
1 small red onion, chopped fine
2 garlic cloves, chopped fine
¼ cup olive oil
1 tablespoon oregano
Salt and pepper
1 tablespoon balsamic vinegar (optional)

Combine all ingredients and pour over fish.

JEROME B. ROBINSON

Jerry Robinson has been traveling and writing about hunting, fishing, camping, conservation and gun dog training for more than 30 years. He wrote for *Sports Afield* for 25 years and in the last 5 years has written for *Field & Stream*. He is the author of two dog training books, *Training the Retriever* and *Hunt Close* which is a guide to training close-working pointing dogs. Both books are now available directly from Jerry in Lyme and have become the "Bible" for training a pointing dog.

His wife Sherrill is a photographer who travels with him frequently and often illustrates his articles. They live on a pond in the woods of Lyme, New Hampshire.

Jerry and Sherry Robinson live in the same town in New Hampshire as we do, and have at least one child who was in high school at the same time as one of ours. When we first moved to Lyme the SC (socially correct) thing to do seemed to be to get rid of whatever fish and game was still in the freezer by asking the Grays and the Robinsons to dinner. I wasn't exactly sure if this was a Yankee form of spring cleaning or simply a desire to pair two hungry couples who might have some basis for conversation. Aside from the sons a year apart in age, there were other similarities: Jerry went to Dartmouth a few years before Ed, both wrote for one of the "big three" outdoor publications and both had wives who happily and professionally needed to accompany them on hunting and fishing trips, both had pointing dogs and both had made life-style choices to stay out of cities.

But as happens in tiny towns (about 1500 souls) the social circle is very small and in a short space of time you've done the circuit several times over. So with the dinner parties dwindling to nothing, our sons going off to college, coupled with the time-consuming and intricate travel schedule of four free-lancers, our relationship soon was reduced to hurried hellos in the grocery store. So we never really have hunted or fished or cooked with Jerry and Sherry. Who could guess what kind of fish recipes they might come up with?

Jerry was in the post office talking to Ed about having just visited his older son, a commercial salmon fisherman in Alaska; how it would be nice to live up there. Or maybe he could marry off Kate (his 14-year-old daughter) to an Inuit and he could live in Labrador. And in the middle of this outdoor writer's fantasy, I interrupted him with my request for a recipe. "Fish? I don't cook fish," Jerry retorted. Uh, oh. I couldn't believe I was going to get some catch-and-release diatribe from Jerry, but who knew? "I eat them raw! I started eating fish this way when fishing with Inuit people in the far north — they just throw you a 3-pound fish at lunch time and expect you to go to work at it with your knife. No fire necessary. I liked it — now eat cold water fish this way regularly." It had been a very long winter in New Hampshire, or may be it was just his train of thought. But then again this is what Jerry sent me a few weeks later:

SASHIMI ON THE ROCKS

1 fillet from an Arctic char, salmon, brook trout, or lake trout
Pinch of salt, or a few drops of lemon juice

The finest sashimi is made from a fish that has just been caught. Simply fillet the fish, removing all small bones. Then slice ⅛" thick in a slanting stoke across the grain. Eat raw fish with a pinch of salt or a few dribbles of lemon juice from a plastic lemon carried in your pack.

SMOKED TROUT

1 lake trout, cleaned thoroughly
¼ cup pickling salt
½ cup brown sugar
Watercress
Hard brown bread

Rub the salt and brown sugar into the cleaned fish and let stand for 4 hours, covered. Rinse in cold water, pat dry with paper towels, then smoke in a Little Chief Smoker for 2 to 3 hours, depending on the thickness of the fish. To serve, split skin along top of back with a thin knife and peel off skin. Serve on a bed of watercress and hard brown bread.

SORREL OR ARUGULA PESTO FOR CHAR

3 cups sorrel or arugula leaves
¼ cup parsley
½ teaspoon sea salt
3 tablespoons olive oil
1 garlic clove

Peel and slightly crush the garlic clove and then add to a quart of boiling water. Blanch the sorrel leaves in the boiling water very briefly and then drain. Combine the blanched leaves and all the other ingredients in a blender or food processor and give it a few zips. Top char, salmon steaks or large trout fillets with spoonfuls of pesto.

JACK SAMSON

In 1970 Jack Samson joined the staff of the then-CBS owned *Field & Stream* magazine and two years later became the editor-in-chief of it, the largest-circulation outdoor publication in the world.

A lifelong fly fisherman, Jack Samson discovered the sport as a boy on the Pecos river near his home in Santa Fe, New Mexico. He became a freelance magazine outdoor writer and for ten years wrote an outdoor column for Associated Press. As editor of *Field & Stream* he fished from Kashmir and East Africa to Scotland and Iceland; from Costa Rica and the Bahamas to Hawaii and Australia. By 1985 when he left *Field and Stream*, Jack had become one of the best-known fly fishermen in the outdoor world. He wrote 16 books on the outdoors while at CBS and has been on the masthead as editor-at-large or fly fishing editor for such publications as *Western Outdoors*, *Marlin Magazine*, and *Fly Rod & Reel*.

In 1988 Jack set a new world record for roosterfish on a fly. And then in 1989 won the First International Billfish Fly Tournament at Flamingo Beach in Costa Rica. He has caught both Pacific and Atlantic sailfish and five species of marlin on a fly, the only man in the word to have done so.

Today Jack lives in Santa Fe with his artist wife, Victoria, and continues to fish and write books. His third book for Stackpole Press, *Permit on a Fly* was most recently published in March, 1996.

Jack Samson is someone Ed and I have known, and known about, for many years now. Like many of us, Jack has juggled his way through life with a split personality; that of the New York City, suit and tie editor versus the Tarponwear™, booted fishing maniac. We met Jack at an art opening in Manhattan in the late 1970s doing the white wine and studied-stare saunter through the King Gallery. There was no question he was accustomed to succumbing to the demands of urban protocols; but his posture definitely signaled a kind of bored tolerance of the situation. And the conversation only became truly animated when the fishing talk started. It was clear that the personality scale tipped to the outdoorsman side with Jack; but it was not until years later that his manic passion was revealed.

Ed and I were fishing the flats near the island of Guanaja, off the coast of Honduras. We were in pursuit of bonefish, of course, but more importantly for the very-tricky permit fish. Our guide was Robert Hyde. Robert had been Jack's guide for many years and had learned much of his guiding knowledge from the master.

Ed had caught a permit, his first ever on a fly, the previous day with Robert's expertise and I was thinking it was my turn. But the day was windy, and the permit seemed to have left the flat where we'd been so lucky before. I thought maybe a new flat, maybe a flat on the other side of the island that would be in the lee of the land would give me an opportunity at a permit. In fact, I'd wondered why we hadn't been over to the other side of the island before, it seemed we'd always fished on the flats on the hotel side. I knew there were flats on the other side because we'd scuba dived there. Robert shook his head when I asked. "No, no," he said, "no one fishes over there. It is very hard to get to, takes many hours to get there and the little boat makes the trip very wet and uncomfortable. No one goes there" – long pause – "except Jack Samson." I wasn't sure that he would have told me that any one went there except that he knew I was an acquaintance of Jack's and might find out. But, of course, this information did nothing but make us both very determined, me to go and Robert to not go. I don't usually lose these arguments.

I never did get to the other side of the island. And I was never quite certain if Robert's reluctance was from fear of the trip or fear of having disclosed the master's prime permit spots.

I do know Jack is quite protective of his permit. When I telephoned him to ask for a recipe for this book, I mentioned we had been fishing for permit with Robert. Perhaps I shouldn't have made the request and mentioned the permit fishing in the same breath; for there was this moment of horrified silence and Jack said, "Eating a permit would be like eating a brother to me!" No, no Jack, I would never eat a permit either! I only want a simple wahoo recipe. Well, maybe I would like another favor; could you let Robert take me to the other side of the island . . . just for a few casts?

THE ABORIGINAL FISH RECIPE

1 fillet from a wahoo, dolphin, red snapper, or sierra mackerel
1 lime
1 garlic clove, crushed
4 tablespoons of unsalted butter
Salt and pepper

Melt the butter and add the crushed garlic clove. Paint the fillet with the garlic butter, sprinkle with salt and pepper and squeeze the lime juice all over it. Broil in the oven for 10 minutes to the inch.

JOHN SWAN

John Swan's watercolors first appeared on the cover of *Gray's Sporting Journal* in 1984 and since then John has become a major force in the sporting art world. Named Ducks Unlimited Artist of the Year and the Atlantic Salmon Federation's Artist of the Year, John has also appeared in such publications as *Esquire Sportsman, Sporting Classics, The Atlantic Salmon Journal, Shooting Sportsman* and *Duck Unlimited* magazine.

His enormously successful one-man shows have been at the American Museum of Fly Fishing and the King Gallery; and he most recently has "illustrated" Tom McGuane's latest book, *Live Water.*

John Swan answered a very big question for me. What ever happened to all those other hippies from the 1960s? I believe John and I are exactly the same age. This means that when he was at the University of New Hampshire studying Art and I was at Boston University studying Journalism we were both living through the remains of the Viet Nam war, Martin Luther King's assassination, Woodstock, a sun in Leo and a moon rising in Cancer (or something equally screwed up), and, of course, Tim Leary and his justifications for alternatives to booze. These were chaotic times on every level imaginable, and the political responsibilities we decided to assume when we were teenagers seemed to supplant the more common and age-appropriate pressure of determining a career path. When we left college a lot of us were into just "being," moving back to the land, growing food organically, living free, etc. That all worked for some longer than it did for both John and me because we both rather spontaneously infused a shot of reality into our lives: marriage and children. Well, some of our generation O.D.'d, some died in Viet Nam, and some committed suicide; and John now bears me out on my theory about the ex-hippies that survived. We're all pretty much grinning along, because we're lucky enough to be making a living from the stuff we studied in school and have loved doing for over 25 years now. How conventional of us!

John still has a few throwbacks to hippie-ism, I can hear it in his talk

– mellow irreverence. He "only paints what he wants to paint," is still "amazed that people actually pay him for his paintings," likes to paint nudes and leaping salmon (not necessarily in one painting), travels to Buffett parrot-head land, but loves his Down East homes in Portland and Rangeley. I was curious to see what John would produce for recipes.

Yup, John's first submission was born of that different drummer with a wry sense of humor. I guess fortuitously, he'd exorcised the organic food syndrome – but less fortuitously mutated into a microwave gourmet of the 1990s. Happily this was not a fish recipe, he wrote, "FRANKFORT POUPON 1) Delicately slice a 'premium' frank diagonally with a silver knife (not plate). 2) Warm the frank 30 seconds (not 25 seconds). Place into a sourdough roll pre-basted with unsalted butter. Generously baste with Country Poupon. 3) Smother entire frank with 1 or 2 slices of Swiss cheese (large holes only). 4) Return to heat source and 'nuke' the hell out of it. 5) Serve with fresh potato chips and 3½ beers. 6) Repeat! Actually a very decent recipe for frankfurters (except he knows I disagree about the 'nuking' time).

Fortunately, John lives with Barb Gould, a woman who owns her own striper fishing boat and who can save him from dying of a diet of radiated dogs and boredom with the following.

SALMON BARBETTE

1 whole salmon, gutted, with skin on (about 3 pounds)
4 tablespoons soy sauce
3 tablespoons brown sugar
2 teaspoons sesame seed oil
½ tablespoon minced ginger
1 – 2 cloves minced garlic

Combine the soy sauce, brown sugar, sesame seed oil, ginger and garlic and rub the mixture all over the salmon including the cavity. Cover and refrigerate several hours or overnight. Grill on an oiled rack over very hot coals for approximately 10 minutes per side or until cooked through. Served over spinach or sautéed greens.

BILL TAYLOR

Bill Taylor is the president and CEO of the Atlantic Salmon Federation, an international, non-profit organization that promotes the conservation and wise management of the Atlantic salmon and its environment. Prior to his appointment as president in November of 1995, Bill was executive director of Communications and Public Policy which involved supervision of the Federation's award-winning publications. Bill has been with ASF since 1988 and also serves on Canada's Atlantic Salmon Advisory Board as Special Advisor to the Canadian Wildlife Federation's Fisheries Committee and on the Coalition on Acid Rain. He is a member of the American Fisheries Society, the Canadian Institute for Environmental Law and Policy and the Canadian Society of Association Executives.

Bill has also written several articles on salmon conservation and has won the prestigious Miramichi Salmon Association Award for journalistic excellence.

Bill Taylor is an Atlantic salmon fisherman, but not exactly. Atlantic salmon fishermen are by-and-large possessed souls. They spend many thousands of dollars a week to fish tiny portions of remote and exclusive rivers only to catch one or less fish. I've seen these fisherman become so crazed about their salmon fishing that they reject all other lower forms of fish, such as trout, wallow in depression and withdraw from reality if they draw the less than optimal week for their fishing. They wax poetic at the salmon's beauty, its ability to fight, its leaps and bounds, its history, its mystique. It is a nice fish. But smallmouth bass jump, too. Have I missed something here?

It's true, I've have only been Atlantic salmon fishing a few times, so perhaps I'm not really one of the initiated. I truly love the Maritime Provinces, the North American places that are home to Atlantic salmon, and I like fly fishing in those big river waters. Of course, I consider the taste of Atlantic salmon unequaled and it has often been the fish's superior flavor that has kept me going during those fishless weeks (years?). But since the environmentally correct thing to do with salmon has come to be to return it to the river, all hope of me becoming a zealot has been lost forever. Alas, I have the heart of a meat fisherman, I guess.

I must confess it was with fear and trepidation that I asked Bill, king of the organization that protects the splendid salmon and a man whose life revolves around those singular souls and their fish, for a recipe. For he probably never fishes for anything but salmon and then never keeps them. Perhaps I have been too harsh in my assessment of the salmon fisherman or perhaps Bill is not quite an Atlantic salmon fisherman. He gave me a trout recipe! (Albeit he fishes for trout only every three or four years.) And, yes, we get to eat salmon — just this once, he says.

WHOLE GRILLED BROOK TROUT

4 brook trout, each about 10" to 12"
2 tablespoons olive oil
4 tablespoons butter
Juice from ½ a lemon
Salt and pepper
½ teaspoon thyme

Clean the trout, leaving on the heads and tails. Combine the olive oil, butter, lemon juice, salt pepper and thyme and sprinkle the mixture inside and out over the trout. Grill the fish over coals for about 8 minutes per side, or until the fish flakes when pricked with a fork.

GRILLED ATLANTIC SALMON IN FOIL

1 5-pound grilse (an Atlantic salmon that has only spent one winter
    at sea)
4 tablespoons butter, melted
Juice of 1 lemon
⅓ cup white wine
Salt and pepper
½ teaspoon thyme
2 shallots, diced

Clean salmon, leaving the head and tail. Combine the melted butter, lemon juice, salt, pepper, thyme and shallots and sprinkle the mixture inside and out over the fish. Place the fish on foil "boat" and pour the wine over the salmon, seal and grill over hot coals for 20 to 25 minutes.

GUY DE LA VALDENE

Guy de la Valdene is a writer and photographer whose elegant little book on the American woodcock, *Making Game*, (Clark City Press, 1990) has become an essential part of the thoughtful upland hunter's library. Guy grew up in the United States and France and his articles have appeared in *Smart, Gray's Sporting Journal, Field & Stream* and other magazines. He is also a contributing editor for *Sports Afield.* He lives with his wife on a farm in northern Florida and just had published *For a Handful of Feathers*, (Grove-Atlantic Press, 1995.)

uy de la Valdene, to me, is a model purveyor of style and thoughtfulness for the angling and shooting world. Guy's just a little older than I, but he'd become a sophisticated practitioner of fly fishing for bonefish and wingshooting woodcock (two sporting endeavors I just now approach competency in) back when I was still shooting bottles with my grandfather's 12-gauge pump gun and catching rock bass off a dock on Lake Michigan. Now he hunts quail and fishes for tarpon, more of my aspirations from the dream-meister.

Then there is his writing: He speaks in poetic truths, and is an incurable romantic; nostalgic, but not bitter — he's delightful and thought-provoking to read. And he cooks. Here's just a simple little recipe, but of course it approaches my concept of fish recipe perfection. It accomplishes delectability through good French-based technique amended with ingredients from the oriental persuasion, my favorite. So with such simpatico between us, touched with my admiration, is there to be more to this relationship?

Probably not, and for one very good reason. Sharks. In an article Guy wrote for *Gray's Sporting Journal* on his years at Deep Water Cay in the Bahamas he describes his first night dive. He writes: "The consensus of opinion was that no one ever encountered sharks after dark. So, girding up our courage, we (Guy and his friend, Gil Drake Jr.) set out on a moonless night, armed with cheap flashlight, my underwater camera, and a four-foot broom handle; we anchored the boat in 15 feet of water, just beyond the barrier reef, and jumped in. The first moment was terrifying and I remember spinning around in the water, hoping to see everything, but granted only a small cone of grace. Five minutes later a five-foot lemon shark swam into our faces . Back to back we tried keeping him in sight, while he kept at least one of his black eyes on us. The standoff lingered, punctuated by hysterical nervous laughter on our part and curiosity on his. Finally I made the mistake of aiming the camera and taking his picture. The flash blinded all present, infuriating the shark so that he raced about, biting everything he could get his teeth into . . . Mirth forced a great deal of water into our lungs and tears from our eyes, but fear came later and was washed down with one of my first tropical drinks. Eventually we dove again, and soon found pleasure in doing so again, without flashlights."

Key phrases here for me are "biting everything he could get his teeth into," "but fear came later," and "Eventually we dove again." And these reactions came from the person who'd written two paragraphs before that early in his experiences he'd learned, " a good shot (spear-fishing) would paralyze 'cuda, sharks didn't die easily, and it was best to mind your appendages." No kidding!

Now it is true that it took only that one clearly "Hollywoodized" scene from "Jaws" to end my long and illustrious skinny-dipping career forever, that learning to scuba dive took me two tries for open-water certification, and the poor woman who was my buddy on my first night dive may never have fully regained the circulation in her hand. But I do believe Guy's joy, courage (stupidity) and fortitude in night diving with sharks to be considerably beyond me . . . and most normal folks. And I have zero desire to learn more about this personality (quirk).

So the chances are probably pretty good that Guy's and my relationship will remain a kiss, kiss hello, a conversation about new and interesting woodcock recipes, what writer is going to which publisher and, perhaps if I'm very lucky, a culinary soirée together on the best method to cook . . . shark.

COBIA DE LA VALDENE AND HAWAII

1 small cobia or mullet, gutted and with head and tail removed
1 quart water
½ cup dry white wine
Juice of 1 lemon
½ teaspoon salt
½ tablespoon tarragon
¼ tablespoon basil
Several pink and green peppercorns
½ cup peanut oil
3-4 cloves of garlic, minced
1 tablespoon (or equal amount to garlic) of fresh ginger root,
    minced
3-4 tablespoons soy sauce

Combine the water, wine, lemon juice, salt, herbs and peppercorns in a fish poacher and bring to a boil, let simmer for 5 minutes. Place the fish in the poacher and let it steam for about 8 minutes (8 minutes per pound) and then remove. Let the fish cool and remove the skin by rubbing your hand across the fish gently. In a small pot, bring the oil to a boil and add the ginger, garlic and soy sauce. It will flare up and spit when you do this, immediately swirl it about and then pour over the cobia and serve.

CHARLES F. WATERMAN

Charley Waterman says in his autobiography, "I am exactly what I wanted to become when I was seven years old. Since seven year olds are not noted for mature judgment and sometimes aspire to piracy or gunfighting, this is not necessarily the pinnacle of success." Charley Waterman is a freelance outdoor writer who has been highly successful in his writing career for over 60 years.

He has written for over 50 newspapers and magazines: *The San Mateo Times, Fort Scott Tribune, Jacksonville Times-Union, Saltwater Fisherman, Gray's Sporting Journal, Sports Afield, Field & Stream, Outdoor Life, Fishing World, Orvis News, Fly Fisherman, Gun Dog, Trailer Travel, Montana Outdoors*; to name only a very few.

Charley has written over 15 books including *The Practical Book of Trout Fishing, The Treasury of Sporting Guns, Hunting in America, The Part I Remember, Fishing in America, Gun Dogs & Bird Guns*, and *Times and Places, Home and Away* (his autobiography).

In addition to this extensive writing career, Charley was a WWII Navy combat photographer, newspaper reporter, a professional wrestler, and a Depression-era boxcar rider — and those were just his vocations. He has traveled throughout the world hunting and fishing. Charley has now appeared in *Gray's Sporting Journal* more than any other writer, including Ed and Becky Gray.

Charley and Debie Waterman have been, very logically, mentors for Ed and me for quite a few years now. We realize this mentor business can be a pretty heavy burden to some people and we've recently tried to protect Charley and Debie from the wear and tear of mentoring by not letting on how important they are to us — and we've actually tried not communicating with them real often.

I wrote about one of my first conversations I had with Charley (now a very long time ago, before we worried about burdening them) in my cookbook, *Gray's Wild Game Cookbook*, written in 1983, "Several years ago our very well-known writer friend, Charley Waterman, came to visit us. So knowledgeable, so lucid, so funny, he was the ideal for the role of hunter/writer mentor. Not that I was either a hunter or a writer, but at that point I sure aspired to be. I could have easily spent every waking moment beside Charley listening to his stories and never tire of it. Driving through the streets of Boston, I picked his brain about everything from the anti-hunters and the rationale for killing to how a husband goes about teaching a wife to enjoy hunting. I had saved my favorite topic for last, wishing to savor the subject and perhaps take notes: Cooking Game. What was Charley's favorite recipe, how long did Charley and Debie cook a duck, how long did they hang their venison for? It all came spewing forth to get the simple reply, "We don't do much of anything to our game, just cook it."

Well, it had been more than 15 years since that conversation and there hadn't really been a whole lot of additional conversations on the topic of fish or game cooking during that time, us trying so hard not to burden them and all. So it was with a bit of shyness that I contacted them requesting a recipe for this cookbook. I sent a letter and got no reply and then apprehensively telephoned, and Charley answered, "We don't do much of anything to our fish, just cook it. We thought you'd want something fancy." Well, this all kind of had a familiar ring to it. But then again ultimate truths do ring.

And what's the ultimate truth ringing here? That uncomplicated and straightforward, whether in a recipe or in people, is ideal. A fresh caught snook simply doesn't need a whole lot done to it to taste great.

Oh, and Charley and Debie are the very best people. I wish I was fishing with them right this minute. I enjoy their company, they know what's important in life and they've always been that way. It's just as simple as that.

ROD AND GUN CLUB SNOOK

1 snook fillet, skin and bones removed
1½ cups cracker meal
1 egg
2 tablespoons milk
2 garlic cloves, chopped
Salt and pepper (red and black pepper) to taste
Oil to cover skillet

Beat together the milk and the egg. Cut serving-size pieces of snook and dredge in the cracker meal and then in the milk/egg mixture. Repeat the dredging in cracker meal. Place the pieces of snook on a platter in single layers separated by waxed paper. Refrigerate, covered, for 6 to 8 hours or more to chill. When mealtime, fry snook pieces in medium-hot oiled skillet about 4 minutes for each side. When turning fish do not use a fork (as the fish will fall apart), once turned season with the salt, peppers and garlic. Fish is done when it flakes. Serve with tartar sauce.
For snook with live-weight of over 6 pounds, the thick section of the fillet should be split before cooking. Other firm-flesh species of fish can be used as a substitute for this recipe.

DILLED SALMON

1 salmon fillet
2 tablespoons oil
1 teaspoon chicken bouillon granules
2 tablespoons dill weed fresh or dry
2 cloves garlic
Pepper to taste
6 tablespoons lemon juice

Heat a large skillet on medium and put in oil and sprinkle with half of the bouillon. Add half of the garlic and half of the dill and place the salmon fillet back down to cook for 3 to 4 minutes. Turn and repeat seasoning on top and cook another 3 minutes. Slowly pour in the lemon juice and let the fish simmer in it 2 to 3 minutes. Serve.

TED WILLIAMS

Ted Williams shares an obsession with fishing, but definitely not baseball, with the 'real' (or as he prefers, 'elder') Ted Williams. Ted the Younger has been writing full time on environmental issues, with special attention to fish and wildlife conservation, for 26 years. In addition to freelancing for national magazines, he contributes feature-length conservation columns to *Audubon* and *Fly Rod & Reel*.

He has been named to the Jade of Chiefs, the highest conservation award given by the Outdoor Writers Association of America. And for his reporting on federal forest-fire policy the American Society of Magazine Editors voted *Audubon* magazine one of five finalists in the National Magazine Awards.

He lives in Grafton, Massachusetts with his wife Donna, Environmental Coordinator for the Worcester Office of the Massachusetts Audubon Society and their daughter, Beth. Their son, Scott, is in environmental studies at Connecticut College.

Ted Williams and I first met when we were in journalism school together at Boston University, he a graduate student and I an undergrad. I took his strong self-confidence and authoritative expertise about certain issues to be the mark of an older, more accomplished journalist. It was not until much later when Ted wrote and edited regularly for *Gray's Sporting Journal*, that I realized when it came to environmental issues such self-confidence and knowledge actually came from being a zealot. This was acceptable, of course, although at times I found it rather frightening.

Then one time, when I was pregnant with my second child, Ted bounded into my office at *Gray's* and thrust in front of me a zip-lock bag full of beautiful, delicate little native brook trout. "Here," he said. We both knew native brook trout were a hard commodity to come by in the hatchery-filled, sometimes industrially polluted and always over-fished streams of New England. Actually I was a bit surprised that not only would he kill these precious and environmentally strained trout, but that he would give them up to me. "Fresh brookies make women fertile and their babies strong; these trout taste the best," said Ted grinning with his usual emphatic confidence. I guess I wasn't sure if Ted had noticed, fertility was not an issue for me at that time. But he was certainly accurate about the big, strong baby (my always big, baby boy has now grown to be over 6'1" and 200 pounds). More importantly, Ted was particularly accurate about the taste of these wonderful little trout. I cooked the brookies in just a little butter. And the gift was a taste sensation that I still recall and savor.

Ted is a fanatic about many environmental issues, particularly when it comes to fish and wildlife conservation. And perhaps this is what makes him so directed when it comes to eating fish properly. Wasting fish is not in his repertoire. He is not a gourmet cook, but he's knowledgeable when it comes to matching the right cooking techniques to the right fish and making them all taste great. And sometimes he even knows to be discerning when he's catching fish; clearly he knew what trout tasted the best. I believe he knows about other fish, too.

BLUEFISH HASH

1 bluefish fillet, cooked
3 large-size potatoes
4 tablespoons unsalted butter
½ pound bacon
1 medium-size onion, finely chopped
½ cup olive oil
Salt and pepper

Bluefish is one of those fish that should never be frozen. It is too oily to be helped by the freezer; to taste right it needs to be very fresh, with the black meat scraped off. Unless you intend to use it for hash. Broil a bluefish fillet or use leftover cooked bluefish (a minimum of 2 cups). Make mashed potatoes by boiling the peeled and quartered potatoes until soft (about a half an hour). Drain, reserving the cooking water. Whip the potatoes, and 2 tablespoons of the butter, adding a little bit of the cooking water at a time until they look like mashed potatoes. Add the fish and the chopped onion. Now fry the bacon until crisp and crumble into the potato-fish mixture. Blend together and check to see if salt or pepper is needed. Form into pancakes and fry in the same pan that cooked the bacon, pouring off the grease, in the olive oil and 2 tablespoons of butter.

RITZ-Y YELLOW PERCH

4-6 small yellow perch
1 cup milk
1 cup finely crumbled Ritz crackers
¼ pound (1 stick) unsalted butter
Juice from ½ lemon
Salt and pepper

Clean and remove the heads and fins of the perch and then scissor out the rib cage level with the backbone. Soak the fish in milk for half an hour and then dredge in the Ritz crackers. Place in a low casserole dish and sprinkle the perch with salt, pepper and the lemon juice. Place the stick of butter on top of the fish and place in a preheated oven at 400° for 15 minutes.

ED GRAY

Ed Gray learned about hunting and fishing while in college and graduate school at Dartmouth. For the next ten years he would mark time working as an officer in the U.S. Navy, an accountant at Price, Waterhouse in Boston, and as Chief Financial Officer for first a computer software company and then for *Sail* magazine. During those ten years he read voraciously about the advocations he had come to love at Dartmouth and decided to make hunting and fishing part of his vocation. In 1975 his life and mine coincided and we started *Gray's Sporting Journal.*

During his 16 years as editor of *Gray's Sporting Journal,* we also started GSJ Press, a sporting travel business, a sporting art catalog, and an outfitter and guide directory entitled *The Guides Book.* In addition, in 1985 Ed and I initiated a "skunk works" relationship with TIME, Inc. and produced two prototype publications, *Sports Illustrated for Kids,* launched in 1986 and a travel-golf publication, *Distant Green.*

In 1989 we sold *Gray's Sporting Journal* to Morris Communications of Augusta , Georgia, and in 1991 left the company. Since that time he has been a freelance writer with articles most frequently in *Men's Journal* and *Sports Afield.* He is a contributing editor of *Sports Afield* and has recently authored the first in a five-book series for Willow Creek Press entitled *Flashes in the River* and is currently completing the second, *Wings from Cover.*

Ed has five children, Caroline, Douglas, Hope, Sam, and Will. We live in Lyme New Hampshire with the youngest son, Will.

E d Gray is my husband and it probably seems a bit odd to those who don't know us to include him in my book. But he is one helluva fisherman and where there's any deficiency in cooking ability, perceived or real, his wife's passion for fine food compensates and can make them a great team effort, as is often the scenario for the Ed Grays. And Ed has some good instincts about cooking as evidenced in his story here. He surely tried to adhere to the French chefs' doctrine of cooking fish whole, rather than in steaks or fillets, as that produces a better tasting fish — this I'm certain he was aware of when trying to cook Ron Rau's 40-pound salmon whole. Well, the guy really does know how to grill.

Some of the best things in life you get to do only once. On a beach in Massachusetts I once grilled a whole, fresh, 40-pound king salmon that had arrived from Alaska as checked baggage two days previous. And while I'm not ruling out a recurrent episode, this event seems surely to remain as singular in the cooking as it was in every other respect.

Our friend Ron Rau, a commercial Alaskan salmon troller and one of the finest writers ever to appear in *Gray's Sporting Journal,* is as free a spirit as you'll likely meet. When he came to visit us in the small beach house we were renting just north of Boston, he hadn't mentioned that his luggage would consist of a day pack and a carefully-packed and insulated, 50-pound waxed carton with one salmon inside. The box was five feet long.

"It'll never fit in our freezer," I said.

Ron's fairly wild-eyed all the time, but his look took on an Old Testament demeanor that I hadn't seen before. "Freezer?" he outraged.

The only answer was a short-notice party. On the way home from the airport we bought 100 pounds of bagged ice cubes, told the kids to use the other shower for a couple days and iced down the salmon in the back bathtub. Two nights later a dozen of our friends showed up to meet Rau and to feast on fresh Pacific salmon.

Hmmm. Now what?

Actually we had worked it out, except for one detail. The answer was to adapt an old New England tradition, the clambake. Rau and I dug a six-foot-long trench in the dry sand above the tide line, lined the hole with aluminum foil and dumped in 40 pounds of charcoal briquettes. Then we went into the kitchen to raid the oven for its grill racks.

"Guess again," said Becky. "I'm cooking the other stuff in there."

Hmmm again. To aid our thinking, Rau went to the refrigerator and got two beers. He just stood there with the door open, doing nothing. I looked at him. He stared into the frig, then turned to me with a raised eyebrow. Eureka.

The refrigerator looked fairly weird with all the food piled on the bottom like that, but we were rich with grill racks now. As I said, it was a rented house.

After that it was pretty straightforward. The people arrived. We fired up the charcoal, and when the coals were glowing like a medieval armorer's forge, we set the refrigerator racks across them just above the flames, put the fish down on the racks and covered the hole thing with a layer of aluminum foil to reflect the heat back down.

We had no idea how long to cook it. After a half hour or so, armed with two garden spades as spatulas and fielding a predictable amount of ill-informed advice from the onlookers, Rau and I flipped the fish. It broke in half, drawing a few boos and catcalls from the riffraff, but turning out to be a serendipitous event that gave us a direct look at how well done the interior flesh was. It wasn't. So we left it on for another half hour until the coals were burning down and the crowd was turning surly, and we served it up.

It was spectacular. We ate it under the stars, right there on the beach, with a light surf running and many toasts to the beautiful, migratory fish and the equally migratory if not so beautiful guy who brought it with him.

INDEX OF RECIPES